BURN
BRIGHT

Inspiring | Educating | Creating | Entertaining

Brimming with creative inspiration, how-to projects, and useful information to enrich your everyday life, Quarto Knows is a favorite destination for those pursuing their interests and passions. Visit our site and dig deeper with our books into your area of interest: Quarto Creates, Quarto Cooks, Quarto Homes, Quarto Lives, Quarto Drives, Quarto Explores, Quarto Gifts, or Quarto Kids.

10 9 8 7 6 5 4 3 2 1

ISBN: 978-1-63106-711-2

Library of Congress Control Number: 2020948975

Publisher: Rage Kindelsperger
Creative Director: Laura Drew
Managing Editor: Cara Donaldson
Senior Editor: John Foster
Cover and Interior Design: Evelin Kasikov

Printed in China

This book provides general information on various widely known and widely accepted practices that tend to evoke feelings of strength and confidence. However, it should not be relied upon as recommending or promoting any specific diagnosis or method of treatment for a particular condition, and it is not intended as a substitute for medical advice or for direct diagnosis and treatment of a medical condition by a qualified physician. Readers who have questions about a particular condition, possible treatments for that condition, or possible reactions from the condition or its treatment should consult a physician or other qualified healthcare professional.

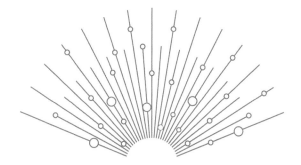

BURN BRIGHT

HEAL YOURSELF FROM BURNOUT AND LIVE WITH PRESENCE, PURPOSE & PEACE

CHARLENE RYMSHA, LCSW

ROCK POINT

Contents

Chapter 4

Chapter 5

Chapter 6

What Is Burnout and Do I Suffer from It?

Life doesn't have to be so hard. I can recall so many instances where some event was coming up or something had to be done, and I felt paralyzed from the inside out. A subtle "stuckness," that complicated the matter, far beyond what was necessary. We as humans are very good at overcomplicating life. In fact, our evolved brains are SO good at thinking that we can *think* ourselves into anything—but thinking ourselves out of jams gets tricky and can lead to burnout.

Burnout is like thinking ourselves into a corner with no foreseeable way out. So, we keep pushing into that corner, hoping it will eventually budge, but all the while feeling more and more exhausted. Yet, if you're willing to take a step back, look around at your options, and apply a different tactic, a new potential is possible.

The thing about "feeling stuck" is that you think you'll always be this way. It tricks you into believing there is NO other possible way to be: *This is my life. There's no wiggle room. I'm stuck.* Every day is the same drudgery. Here's the thing, though: you feel stuck because that has become your habitual way of being—your perceived reality. But you can change habits. Small and subtle shifts, done with conscious choice and consistency, create big change. In this book, you'll be guided through a change process that will help you learn to resolve old ways of thinking, feeling, and doing that have made your life harder.

It's helpful to start by recognizing burnout as your wake-up call to course correct. You didn't choose for your life to feel exhausting or disconnected, yet here you are. The good news is you've simply lost sight of how you truly want to live and who you really are, and this can be remedied, because the answers to how you want to live and who you really are already reside within you.

The vibrant, energetic, fun, interesting, passionate, ambitious, driven person that you are still exists—it's just time to deconstruct and reorganize your reality so that it aligns with the best version of you.

I honor you for picking up this book and making the decision to change. You can expect to experience growing pains along the way, since true healing requires letting go of the "known" and stepping into the "unknown." The brain gets scared when it doesn't know what to expect; therefore, I designed this book so that the chapters build upon each other, scaffolding to the next level. As you learn to deeply trust yourself in this process, your perspective will shift from fear to excitement. You're already ambitious and want the best out of life—I can help you get there without the added stress that leads to burnout.

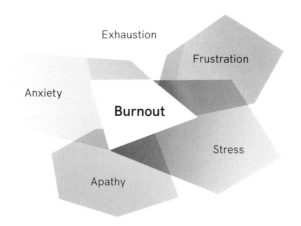

Exhaustion

Frustration

Anxiety

Burnout

Stress

Apathy

What Is Burnout?

Burnout has become status quo for a remarkable number of people. Yet it still remains a hidden epidemic. In some very real ways, burnout is the art of projecting that you're "OK," "life is great," "everything's fine," while feeling broken down inside. Since much of the experience of burnout occurs internally, the extent of the suffering is invisible. You may look around your office and think that everyone else is holding it together and wonder, with mild panic and self-judgment, *What's wrong with me?* There's nothing wrong with you; you're just burnt out! (And it's most likely that many of your coworkers are, too.) You can begin the recovery process by first understanding what burnout is.

In May 2019, the World Health Organization (WHO) announced "burnout" as a medical syndrome, defining it as a workplace phenomenon due to mismanaged stress. The fact that burnout is considered a syndrome means it can be identified by a cluster of symptoms that are typically experienced together. These clusters vary from person to person, meaning that each person's presentation of burnout is unique. Your burnout may look and feel very different from that of your coworkers, and like all medical and mental health conditions, the symptoms are identifiers of underlying factors that are contributing to a heightened level of distress. Before we can dive into the deeper reasons behind burnout (which will be explored throughout this book), you must first become aware of your blend of burnout symptoms. The following checklist in Exercise 1 will help you do just that.

BURNOUT SYMPTOMS SELF-ASSESSMENT

Objective:

To determine whether, and in what ways, you're experiencing burnout.

Time + Frequency:

Ten minutes; one time (again for reassessment at the end of your burnout journey [see Exercise 35 on page 147]).

Directions:

Review the checklist and check off any and all that apply to you.

○ I'm totally exhausted most of the time.

○ I feel overwhelmed by my mounting to-do list and competing priorities.

○ I feel constantly busy, yet I feel like I'm achieving less than I should.

○ I experience anxiety or low-grade panic.

○ I struggle with work-life balance and have little personal time, even for friends and family.

○ I'm becoming increasingly irritable, annoyed, angry, and short-tempered.

○ I'm under a crushing amount of pressure to succeed.

○ I'm increasingly cynical or hypercritical toward myself and others.

○ I have trouble either falling asleep or staying asleep.

○ I find it hard to concentrate and stay on task.

○ Life has become a bunch of tasks to get done, and I'm losing all sense of purpose.

○ I've been drinking and/or eating too much (or perhaps, eating too little).

○ I worry a lot about work, people, and the future and/or the past.

○ I suffer from digestion problems, tension headaches, and/or chronic aches and pains.

Please note that this isn't an exhaustive list or a diagnostic test but a self-awareness tool that will help you understand what burnout currently looks and feels like for you. Throughout this book, you'll gain a deeper understanding of your burnout and practical ways to heal from what you have going on.

Although burnout is classified as a "workplace phenomenon," it doesn't start and stop during business hours. This is for numerous reasons, including the increasingly blurred boundaries between work life and personal time. And for some people, work is not the root of their stress. But, stress is less about where it comes from and more about how you choose to handle what it is that's stressing you out.

Most of us mismanage stress because we haven't been taught how to manage it in the first place. There's no stress management course as

standard school curriculum (yet), and as a culture we're pretty unaware of the healthy ways to manage stress. So, we all make do, creating coping strategies to get by, and we use them until they stop working. In this way, burnout starts to become apparent when our coping strategies fall short of our ability to suppress our accumulated stress.

Burnout is the culminating result of a depletion of internal resources due to chronic and ongoing stress, leaving you tired, despondent, and joyless. I often hear it described as mental, emotional, and physical exhaustion. This experience makes total sense, since chronic stress effectively cuts off clear communication between all systems in the body and mind, leading to lowered capacity to function.

The Science Behind Burnout

Your nervous system is your internal stress management system. When burnt out, this system malfunctions and stress stays with you and becomes your normal way of living. Specifically, stress management is handled within the autonomic nervous system with two modes of operation: (1) parasympathetic and (2) sympathetic. Only one can be "on" at a time, and they are designed to work in harmony so that you can rest and recover in order to take action as needed, creating a balance of "rest" and "action" to properly regulate your whole body-mind system.

The autonomic nervous system is part of our ancient evolution and is essential to survival. The *parasympathetic nervous system* is your rest-and-recovery mode. When you're in this stage, you feel relaxed, safe, and available for yourself and other people in your life. Your immune, digestive, respiratory, cardiac, lymphatic, adrenal, and all other systems within your body are functioning well and doing their jobs to help you self-heal and thrive. This is where humans are designed to live most of the time.

The *sympathetic nervous system*, on the other hand, is your survival response, intended to turn on temporarily when you're in a life-threatening situation and then return you to baseline of rest-and-recovery when the threat has receded. This system was highly useful and necessary back in primitive times in order to keep our species alive. Picture this: you're a cave person, functioning in parasympathetic mode. You're aware of your surroundings, yet you're not on high alert. Then a saber-toothed tiger jumps out of the bushes, and your body switches into sympathetic mode before you can even consciously register the threat. It immediately chooses one of the three options: (1) fight, (2) flight, or (3) freeze. You either wrestle the tiger, run away, or play dead. Once you've survived the threat, meaning the tiger has left and you're still alive, your body returns to the parasympathetic mode of rest-and-recover.

Humans are still biologically wired this way. Your sympathetic nervous system turns on when you perceive a threat and then returns to parasympathetic when the threat has passed. In our modern society, perceived threats come at you from every angle, multiple times per day. Whether it's the ten emails that hit the inbox in the last forty-five seconds or an influx of deadlines and competing demands from the people in your life, you're fending off perceived threats every day. And unlike the occasional real-life saber-toothed tigers of times past, these perceived threats are constantly lurking and ready to pounce. So, in order to be ready for anything that comes your way, your body and mind remains in "survival mode."

The sympathetic nervous system works in tandem with the reptilian part of the brain. The reptilian brain is much less evolved than the logical prefrontal cortex, so each of these modern-day perceived threats registers as life threatening. Now, the higher functioning portion of your brain, the prefrontal cortex, knows that the email you just received does not put you in imminent danger. Yet, the reptilian part of your brain, primarily the amygdala, is quicker to respond and registers this information as *I might die*, signaling your body and mind to react accordingly.

Burnout is when your body and mind are on constant high alert and you're perpetually in survival mode. That sense of being "always on" is an activated sympathetic nervous system. Your body and mind have forgotten how to return to the parasympathetic mode of rest-and-recovery. Cortisol, the main stress hormone, floods your body, ensuring that you stay *on* and don't rest. Rest would mean death to your reptilian brain. High levels of cortisol are linked to short-term problems, such as your burnout symptoms in Exercise 1 (see page 10)

and long-term health risks, such as heart disease, type 2 diabetes, lowered ability to manage weight, and hormone imbalances, to name a few.

Modern Stress "Tigers"

You already know that it doesn't feel good to be stressed all the time. Let's take a moment and identify some of your everyday saber-toothed tigers, those situations that trigger your survivalist stress response. Think about your average day and ask yourself what are some things that heighten your stress levels. Is it your commute to work? Is it the moment you walk into the office? Is it each alert on your phone? Is it the expectations of others? These are just a few examples of common stress tigers, and yours are unique to you. In Exercise 2, you will learn what your saber-toothed stress tigers are so that you can begin to mitigate your stress response.

YOUR STRESS TIGERS

Objective:

Awareness is the first step to managing your stress tigers. This exercise will help you identify what stresses you out and your body's automatic reactions to them.

Time + Frequency:

Fifteen minutes; add (or remove) stress tigers as your awareness builds.

Directions:

STEP 1: Think about a normal day for you. Start by thinking of the morning as you wake up and mentally "walk" yourself through your day until you go to bed.

STEP 2: What situations bring on stress? Each situation is a stress "tiger" of yours.

STEP 3: Use the following list of common arenas where stress lurks and write down your specific ones.

AT HOME:
Example: When your alarm goes off in the morning.

YOUR COMMUTE:
Example: Heavy traffic that's making you late (again!).

AT WORK:
Example: Boss calls you into her office.

FRIENDS/FAMILY/PARTNER:
Example: Text from a close friend you haven't seen in a while asking you to come out for drinks tonight.

FINANCIAL:
Example: Email reminder that your student loan payment is due.

SOCIAL MEDIA:
Example: The forty DMs you haven't responded to.

OTHER:
Example: Sitting alone at a coffee shop, pondering what you're doing with your life.

Now, think of one of these stress tigers and take note of your body's reaction to it. Did your palms start to sweat? Did your heart begin to beat faster? Did your stomach tighten? These are some ways your body can respond to stress. It's important to recognize these stress tigers so that you can begin to loosen their grip on your life. This book will go into greater detail on how to release their hold in a way that resets your baseline to a parasympathetic mode so you can effectively handle life's stressors with greater ease.

Starting today, begin to notice when a stress tiger shows up. Identify what the stress is and how your body alerts you to it. When you are in this state, take a few breaths to begin the calming process, and with your higher-thinking brain tell yourself the following: *I am safe; I am not dying; This is a perceived threat;* and *This stress is not an actual saber-toothed tiger*. By doing this, you're beginning to create coherence between the body and mind to better understand your stress, regain autonomy over your life, and begin the burnout recovery process.

Burnout Culture

We live in a culture that glorifies everything that keeps you on high alert. There's the pressure to perform and produce as much as you possibly can. Messages that need your constant attention. Being available to everyone at any time, day or night. It's no wonder that nearly everyone is feeling burnt out. This lifestyle of our modern, digitized society is simply not sustainable. As we continue to live this way, there seems to be no way out. Convincing ourselves that this is how business and life in general get done, we resign ourselves to keeping the pace of social expectations.

In this current, on-demand state, "stopping" means you'll get eaten by a saber-toothed tiger, so you simply keep going and push harder to get through each day, as the crippling effects of burnout mount. You begin to notice a lowered return on your investment, which spirals you further into despair. This isn't only happening to you—it's happening to your co-workers and showing up in the bottom line of financial reports. Everyone is scrambling, staving off imminent death, working as hard as they can to keep pace with the madness. Can you relate?

TIP

Aligning more with cultural norms than with who you are on a deeper level contributes to burnout. Fortunately, the opposite is just as true—burnout recovery is a true reclamation of "self" as you get clear on who you are and how you want to live.

But here's the thing, even as the outer world may seem to be in shambles and your internal world is crumbling, you still have a choice. You can recognize that how you are currently dealing with stress is not actually working. By learning to do things in a new, more sustainable way, you can function at a much higher level than you are now. Imagine what life could be like if you learned to slow down, just enough to allow the parasympathetic mode to turn on from time to time to allow your whole body-mind system to shift from survival mode to feeling fully alive. The current social system may be broken, but *you* are not—and you don't need to hit rock bottom to come to this conclusion.

Stop Before You're Forced to Stop

Since burnout is the norm, socially and currently internalized, the drive to just keep going is strong. It's very human to avoid the pain of change until the pain of your current situation becomes too much to ignore. People normally change only when they're forced to do so. I can assure you that the rock bottom of burnout is more painful than the courage it will take to start making changes in your life today. If you wait, burnout can result in the inability to function in any normal capacity and life as you know it will abruptly change.

Being forced to stop due to burnout typically occurs in one of two ways: (1) the symptoms become so severe that you are mentally, emotionally, and physically depleted to the point of total exhaustion and you are unable to get out of bed, and/or (2) you suffer a severe physical injury due to the effects of burnout. The most famous example of the latter is Arianna Huffington's accident in which, due to what she described as "sleep deprivation and exhaustion," she passed out and awoke on the floor "in a pool of blood" with a broken cheekbone. It's all too common to ignore the symptoms of burnout, but if you begin to listen to your body and mind, you'll be saved from catastrophic effects of such later stages of burnout.

The feeling of "being stuck" in the rat race or daily grind can create a sense of hopelessness. But the good news is that things can change with awareness and consistent practice. As you begin to shift what's going on inside, you will become better equipped for the world around you. Right now, your nervous system is in survival mode, but wellness is not mere survival. It's about reclaiming who you are beyond the confines of debilitating stress so that you can truly live. Try Exercise 3 to start to reclaim yourself.

RECLAIM YOURSELF

Objective:

These questions are intended to get your mind thinking about reclaiming who you are. When you think it, you can become it. These answers will provide guidance as you find your way back to who you are and how you want to live.

Time + Frequency:

Five to ten minutes; one time (review as needed).

Directions:

Read and consider each question and then write your answers down.

In what ways does stress cut me off from what I know?

Who am I without stress?

Who would I be if stress could be more contained in my life?

Holistic Healing Principles

A holistic approach to burnout recovery, as I'm defining it here, is the process of choosing to value "rest" as much as "productivity" and by aligning your thoughts, emotions, and actions to prioritize this new way of living. As you learn to slow down and be guided by what I call your "Inner Knowing," an entirely new perspective builds, one that will lead you out of burnout. When you feel stressed out, your body and mind have forgotten how to rest, so everything is in high-speed, go mode. Your thoughts are constantly streaming, your emotions are unpredictable, and your body is restless. This is no way to live.

The key is to learn how to value rest without feeling guilty or thinking you're being lazy. This will simply make you more available when action is needed. By choosing to honor rest and allowing yourself to slow down, you're able to recalibrate your body and mind. The quick road to burnout disconnects you from your true potential—and slowing down just the right amount will actually get you to where you want to go. As you learn to quiet your mind, process your emotions, and reset your nervous system, a state of "relaxed alertness" becomes your new baseline.

Unfortunately, there's no shortcut to getting there; it's not a piecemeal type of a process where you treat each symptom on the checklist, take more yoga classes, quit your job, or go on an extended vacation. None of these actions will get to the root of the problem, which is that you're disconnected from who you are and what's truly important to you. As you learn to honor rest, you rebuild the clear connection between body and mind and become a whole, highly functional system again.

Have you ever had the experience when your life just seemed to flow? Those moments when life felt easy, almost effortless, with no stumbling and no fumbling? Innovative ideas and creativity came to you without strain. The people you needed to show up for you did. There was no doubt in what you were doing, and you confidently proceeded. That is what happens when you're connected to your Inner Knowing, which is accessible with practice as you learn to honestly show up for yourself.

All change happens in the present moment, and transforming in a holistic way means doing so with your *whole being*. As you learn to connect with all that you are in the present moment, you become whole and begin to heal. This is done by building a holistic lifestyle through which you become increasingly aware of the present moment of your lived experience by recognizing your current thoughts, feelings, and behaviors. What are you thinking right now? What are you feeling right now? What physical action are you doing right now? As you build your practice to return to the present moment and begin to pay attention to your thoughts, feelings, and actions, you become aware of your habitual ways of moving through the world.

This is when conscious choice becomes possible. Slowing down enough to notice who you are in this very moment gives you the opportunity to practice and learn how to deeply listen to your Inner Knowing, which will guide you into your optimal life—the life you were born to love. Let's look at some holistic healing principles that will help you on your way to burnout recovery.

Mantras

Mantras are positive statements made in the present tense. As you begin to practice making conscious choices that align with your desired life, try Exercise 4 *Three-Word Mantra*. It was inspired by a conversation I had with someone who said, "I have the opposite of burnout." This made me wonder, *What's the opposite of burnout?* This question validates the fact that not only is each person's experience with burnout unique, but their ideas about "not being burnt out" (i.e., wellness) are also unique.

THREE-WORD MANTRA

Objective:

To create a short and positive statement that reinforces your sense of personal wellness.

Time + Frequency:

Five minutes; five times per day for three weeks (until it becomes an automatic thought).

Directions:

STEP 1: What is one word that would describe the opposite of burnout for you? You can select from the list below or add your own. You can even change it tomorrow, so there's no pressure. Simply pick one now.

Ease   Peace   Joy   Fun   Grace

Playfulness   Light   Happy   Relaxed   Funny

Rested   Kind   Love   Simple   Connected

Open   Carefree   Bubbly   Flow   Effortless

Unstoppable   Available   Freedom   Grounded

Now that you have chosen your one word, add it to this phrase:

I choose _____

STEP 2: Say this mantra to yourself three times right now. How does it feel? You may notice that you're having some resistance to the statement with counter thoughts such as, *No I'm not,* or some other automatic thought reaction. Or, maybe you're embracing this experience and feeling the lightness of your mantra. Either way, there is no one right way to do it. This is an awareness practice that begins to reinforce your new choice. I encourage you to repeat your simple three-word mantra as often as possible. And as you do, notice how your emotions and body respond.

Here's where I let you in on a little secret: I believe you can have it all—everything that truly matters to you! It just takes reassessing what "everything" is for you through the process of finding inner balance and allowing your chosen life to expand. You create a balanced life when you intimately know what you want and then prioritize what's most important to you. Fostering your well-being is both a gift to you and those around you, because when you live a balanced life, you shine. And this brightness is contagious, inspiring those around you to seek their own deepening sense of well-being.

Destigmatizing Being Human

You're human, which means you're not impervious to pain, and you will make mistakes, learn from them, and grow stronger. Give yourself permission to be your whole self by recognizing and accepting the human condition.

Yay, you're human! And you have your own brand of the human condition that's equal parts messy and beautiful. It's what makes *you,* and every being on this planet, magnificent. Humans are fascinating in that we are deeply feeling beings with high cognition. This means (among other things) that we have the ability to take things personally. We can be hurt by what someone says or does and adapt our behavior to be less vulnerable to the judgment of others—and it's this protective shield that hinders our healing.

By denying your humanness, you feel more stuck, guilty, shameful, and fearful, and therefore much less like *you*. Our species has evolved to become incredibly good at wearing self-imposed masks, implying that the real person behind the mask is flawed and not good enough. When you begin to work from the premise that we all have issues, your life will start to feel lighter, and you'll no longer need to keep pretending or hiding the fact that you are indeed human.

With this acceptance, the difficult and unique stuff that makes up your variety of the human condition won't be gone overnight, but that sense of heaviness as well as the time and effort spent on hiding, denying, ignoring, and pushing away your truth will fade away. This means you'll have more time and energy to spend on healing the real issues—the things that burn you out.

In the meantime, I invite you to accept that your version of the human condition exists and embrace it! I want you to love all the ways that you've learned to navigate and adapt to where you are today. And, from this place of honoring yourself with compassion and kindness, you can really start to heal.

In fact, the more compassion you give yourself, the faster you'll recover from burnout—and say good-bye to it forever. I'm going to let you in on another secret: there is no "perfect" version of yourself—and the quicker you realize this, the better off you'll be. It's time to course correct by accepting the "real" you instead of spending time and energy creating coping strategies and defense mechanisms to hide your wounds. I'm not suggesting that this will be easy, but it is totally doable, which is why I wrote this book for you.

Why I Wrote This Book

I stepped into my first yoga class in 1995, and that's when my healing trajectory began. Unbeknownst to me at the time, the practice of fully integrating my mind and body for enhanced well-being would become my life's work. Suffering from extremely low self-esteem and a sense that I was irreconcilably broken, I fumbled and foiled on my self-healing path for another few years until one day I realized that I had a choice: I could stay stuck and continue to live each day like it was a chore, or I could decide to "get well."

Although I didn't know what wellness actually looked or felt like, I decided that I was going to figure it out and I set "wellness" as my intention. At that time, I had moved from the East Coast, where I grew up, to Northern California, where I had the great fortune of meeting a therapist who helped me change my life. Her loving presence and healing perspective helped me realize that my negative self-beliefs were not necessarily true—and over time, I learned that I wasn't broken after all. While seeing this therapist, I maintained a consistent yoga and mindfulness practice, along with almost daily extreme sports—I skied in the winter and mountain biked in the warmer months.

The ability to be present with myself and deeply connected to my body, in both easeful practices and fast-paced activities, taught me to equally honor the benefits of both "rest" and "action." Balanced well-being became my reality, and as my connection to my own sense of who I am deepened, so did my relationships. Life became increasingly meaningful as I gained an internal sense of wholeness. My mind quieted of negative self-talk, my emotions became more manageable, and my body's response to stress improved. Through this calmness emerged an effervescent feeling of joy. This energetic resonance—a sense of "Grounded Expansion" (which we will look at more in detail in chapter 2) that was both relaxed and energized at once—became my new normal. Although healing and wellness is a journey that lasts a lifetime, I felt that I had learned enough about wellness to live a self-defined, high-quality life.

Through my own suffering, and coming out the other side, I realized everyone deserves to live the kind of life I achieved. I wanted to give back and offer what I learned about getting well, so I obtained a master's degree in social work and became a therapist. Through my personal healing journey,

formal education, and therapy clients, I came to realize that a holistic approach to wellness is the most effective way to facilitate real change. You can talk all day about what's bothering you, but if you keep the mind separate from the healing powers of the body, recovery is stifled. This is the reason I started my business, Everyday Coherence, from *everyday*, meaning "daily," and *coherence*, meaning "interconnected," and created the Say Goodbye to Burnout program.

The process of regaining coherency is learned through simple and effective strategies that will teach you how to fully integrate your mind and body, reconnecting you to who you really are and enabling the mind-body to self-heal. As coherency is practiced each day, it becomes your new normal. Balance is restored and the effervescent sense of Grounded Expansion becomes attainable at any time, even when you're at work, sitting at the computer writing a report, for example. Using these basic healing tenets, I created the Say Goodbye to Burnout program in response to the pervasiveness of burnout as the modern-day joy-suck that it is. An inner sense of joy is the driving force that sustains my well-being—and I offer this book to you, as a resource to reclaim your joy and live a life that truly matters.

How to Use This Book

This book is designed to be a practical guide to help you do the deep healing work necessary to get out of burnout and into a state of sustainable well-being. Each chapter offers an area of focus that builds on each prior chapter to help you heal and align all aspects of who you are. You'll begin with mindfulness as a concept and practice and then move on to the body and mind. You'll continue to explore emotions, identify social and personal values, and lastly, design a personalized wellness guide to keep you on track to maintaining a burnout-free lifestyle.

As you read, you'll find that each chapter offers information and practical exercises to reinforce what you just learned. This book is not simply a quick read and then you're done; burnout is a big problem that warrants a more intentional, sustained solution. Provided in these pages is a modified "self-led" version of my work with clients. Holding yourself accountable may prove to be your biggest obstacle, but please know I'm with you every step of the way. The real work is in the practice of the exercises, which you will do on a continual basis to create new habits and actual change.

To resolve burnout and kick it forever takes practice, dedication to your healing journey, and a willingness to get uncomfortable at times. Real change doesn't happen overnight or by remaining in your comfort zone. Through this process, you'll use many of your same assets (i.e., ambition, drive, creativity, and the desire to live a truly meaningful and important life) that got you burnt out in the first place, but in a new way that will support your healing and move you into "thrive mode."

Within these pages, you'll find many practice options that you can build into a complete holistic lifestyle tool kit. Consistency and flexibility are key—so go at your own pace, returning to previous chapters when needed for reference, and do the exercises that are most effective for you. As you change, so will your practice. This recovery process and the practices in this book are designed to fit into your already full day, and as you build your daily awareness practice, you'll soon notice that your days will feel less hectic and a lot calmer. The only tools that are necessary to participate in this burnout recovery process are:

- A willingness to be open to the ideas and practice them

- An analog journal to capture self-reflection and personal insights

As an added benefit, check out the About the Author section on page 158 to learn how to access supplemental materials provided in this book.

Unfortunately, there is no magic number of days it takes to recover from burnout, yet most people following these practices experience the healing transformation within six weeks to two months. A recommended time frame to follow the program in this book would be: one week for the introduction and chapter 1 and two weeks each for chapters 2 through 6.

Although there are, what researchers call, evidence-based "best practices," there's no one "right" way to do anything. And there's only one person who knows what's best for you—and, yes that is *you*. This is why I'm sharing what I know about burnout prevention, recovery, and optimal well-being so you can tailor it to your own needs and desires.

The information and exercises in this book are based on my graduate studies and work as a psychotherapist, books I've read, courses I've taken, and guidance from other helping professionals. My own experiences, as well as my clients' positive transformations, are proof that the guidelines in this book can change your life.

Now, let's begin your journey to recover from burnout!

Introduction Summary

Burnout is your wake-up call to do things differently. We as humans tend to create change in our lives once we've finally had enough with our current situation. And when it comes to burnout, it takes great courage to recognize and decide to beat it because there are so many rational reasons to keep going. It's socially acceptable—and even the norm—to keep pushing harder, and it seems that all around you people are handsomely rewarded for functioning at breakneck speed without pausing for self-care or reflection.

Yet your body and mind are telling you a different story, one that recognizes change is needed for sustainable well-being. By choosing to pick up this book, you've already started to make the necessary changes that your future self will thank you for. Burnout has you feeling stuck and life may feel insurmountably hard, but that is not the whole story.

In this introduction, you've learned the signs and symptoms of how burnout shows up in your life, the science behind why you feel "always on," as well as some useful tools and awareness strategies to end burnout and create a life you love. Since the stress "tigers" of burnout can come from many places and affect your whole being, a holistic healing approach is offered within these pages.

As you give yourself permission to be human and inherently imperfect, you're liberated to start from where you are in this very moment and learn how to heal yourself. It's in the *now* that you get to choose healing as your path and start to change. Your mind-set will shift to honor rest, and your actions will slow your pace so you can become aware of your current thoughts, emotions, and behaviors. It's from this place of awareness that all change is possible.

Introduction Skill Take-Aways

Showing up for yourself on a daily basis and consistently practicing the tools and exercises in this book is how you will self-heal. The skills learned in the introduction are your starting-off point, and new skills will be introduced in each subsequent chapter. Let's do a quick recap of the exercises you completed and discuss their take-aways:

- The *Burnout Symptoms Self-Assessment* in Exercise 1 is an awareness tool designed to help you understand the ways that burnout is showing up in your life. As you proceed through this book, you may find it helpful to return to this checklist and reassess your progress.

- Next you identified *Your Stress Tigers* in Exercise 2 in order to build awareness of when they occur and how they feel in your body on a daily basis. You will continue to hone this skill throughout the book as you gain deeper insight into your body and mind's responses to daily triggers, along with strategies to alleviate the stress response.

- You have begun to *Reclaim Yourself* through the prompts provided in Exercise 3 with the intent to remind you of who *you* really are without stress. I hope this was an eye-opening and uplifting exercise for you that will serve as a guide back to the true you.

- By creating your own *Three-Word Mantra* in Exercise 4, you're already gaining clarity on how you choose to feel and move through the world. Mantras are a powerful tool to actively facilitate transformation and reinforce healing principles. I encourage you to keep up with this practice daily, changing out your "wellness term" as you see fit.

Chapter 1

Mindfulness Focus

Mindfulness is the practice of cultivating awareness within and outside of you by placing your attention on one point of focus. This is not a distraction tool, since it hones your ability to be with what actually *is*, in the present moment. Simply being with yourself, quiet and often with eyes closed, can bring up strong feelings of anxiousness as you start to build a mindfulness practice. As you try to quiet down, you may have thoughts like, *How can I possibly be here now, doing nothing, when there is so much to get done?* Taking the time to slow down can feel futile because there's such a strong counter-belief that you need to check off your to-do list NOW. So, NOW is not the time to rest . . . but when is? And to what end—and at what cost?

There is no real "end" to life tasks—the list goes on and on. But when you can slow down, focus, and be present, life becomes a "lived experience" as you move through your day. How different would your life feel if you could stop checking off boxes as quickly as possible and show up alive and ready for whatever comes your way?

Slowing down to get what you want out of life probably sounds like a preposterous idea—or at minimum a nice, yet unattainable, dream. This is because the neurobiology of your brain and autonomic nervous system are currently hardwired to believe and feel this way—convincing you that you must work harder, faster, and relentlessly to reach your goals.

This chapter explores some main reasons why mindfulness can seem like a waste of time (but it's so worth it!), along with scientific studies and observations of highly effective people who have proven otherwise.

The #1 Addiction of Burnout

It's not uncommon to be writing a report, replying to emails, listening to a podcast, answering DMs, and texting all at the same time. Can you relate? There can be a sense of accomplishment in doing all of this at once, which triggers the desire to do more of it. Yet, that's the pull of any addiction—the illusion of perceived benefits without recognizing the downside. This is your addiction to multitasking, or what Shawn Achor, author of *The Happiness Advantage*, calls "cultural ADHD."

You may be thinking, *But I'm a great multitasker*. Yet the truth is that you're not good at multitasking because no one is. A 2009 Stanford University study unintentionally debunked the benefits of multitasking. The study was initially conducted to gauge what high-achieving multitaskers do differently than the general population in order to identify the most efficient ways to do multiple things at once.

However, the research showed that the seasoned multitaskers were worse at task completion than people who tended to take on one thing at a time. Most significantly, the brains of multitaskers were unable to filter out unnecessary information. They had trouble deciding what to focus on and took longer to switch from one task to another. In fact, ongoing and habitual multitasking creates disorganized brain activity that sends the body and mind scrambling for answers on a daily basis.

This sustained disorganization heightens production of the stress hormone cortisol and is a prime culprit of the internal chaos that is experienced as burnout. Multitasking makes you slower; meanwhile, your body and mind are working in overdrive to get everything done faster.

Many other studies on the topic of multitasking from the University of Michigan, Massachusetts Institute of Technology (MIT), and the University of London, to name a few, recognize multitasking as a dangerous and ineffective habit that has been shown to lower IQ and suppress creativity and innovation. In Exercise 5 you will practice focusing your attention on a single task so that you can work smarter, and not harder.

Reward and Repeat

It's easier than you may realize to manipulate your brain to want more. Dopamine, known as the feel-good neurotransmitter, is necessary for brain and body functioning and supports motivation and memory. However, it can be overdone to the detriment of your ability to sustain motivation and focus. Receiving a "dopamine hit" occurs when this brain chemical is released in a large quantity in response to a certain action, providing a sense of euphoria. You naturally want more of this pleasurable state, so you repeat the action. Unfortunately, this reward system is unsustainable and is at the root of many addictions, including drugs, gambling, and yes, multitasking.

MONOTASKING

Objective:

Since multitasking creates a disorganized brain pattern that scatters your focus, when you practice one task at a time, you gain the basic tenets of mindfulness and retrain your brain back into mental clarity.

Time + Frequency:

Two minutes; one time a day for one week (extend as needed).

Directions:

STEP 1: Choose any single task that you already perform in a typical day. Examples include making coffee, brushing your teeth, listening to a podcast, etc.

STEP 2: Engage in that one activity with full focus. This means you're not scrolling through your news feed while brushing your teeth, checking your email while listening to a podcast, or whatever it may be. Place all of your attention on this one action.

STEP 3: Notice any urge you may feel to reach for something else to do and then return your attention to the one task.

Advanced Versions*

To advance this practice and skill level, you can (1) add more time to your monotask, or (2) practice this exercise at another point in the day when you notice you're multitasking. The practice would then be to stop everything that you're doing and choose to do only one thing at that time.

To further advance this exercise, review your day's to-dos, decide what sequence to perform them in, and do one item at a time. If something unexpected pops up, such as a call from your top customer, temporarily suspend what you're doing and place your full attention on the customer.

The advanced versions are to be attempted only when you have practiced the exercise and feel confident in your ability to complete it with minimal distractions.

And, here's the kicker: there's no such thing as multitasking. Yes, you can do more than one thing at a time, but your brain is only able to focus on one thing at a time. Meaning, when your brain multitasks, it toggles its circuitry between each of the tasks. With more tasks comes more switching, which promotes cognitive fatigue and leads to the mental exhaustion you may feel halfway through the day.

The word "multitasking" originated as a computer term, which described the ability to process two or more jobs at the same time. After a while, it became a term used to describe human behavior. But we humans will never be as fast and efficient at data processing as a computer, yet we continue to speed up as if we're machines—and even if we could function like robots, technology isn't immune to burnout. At times, devices need to be turned off, rebooted, and plugged into a sustainable energy source in order to remain functional. The more programs that are running at once, the slower the computer becomes, and it may even freeze or shutdown. Think of human burnout as having too many tabs open, which leads to cloudy brain fuzz, brain freeze, and shutdown. If your body and mind are worn down too much, burnout can feel like having a dead battery that won't hold a charge.

The Drive to Be Productive Is Not So Productive

Productivity is a common measure of work performance that has a cause-and-effect: the more hours you put in, the higher the output. However, like the myth of multitasking, hyperproductivity is killing your results. Studies and productivity experts agree that there's a cap to how much work you can put in and how productive you can be. Particularly in our age of "knowledge working," meaning a job in which output is thought-produced, you can be productive four to six hours per day. Beyond that, productivity declines and cognitive fatigue rises.

TIP

You may not be able to convince your boss to grant you a thirty-hour work week (with the same salary), but you can use your energy more efficiently at work by taking mini-breaks throughout the day. Even standing up and moving around for five minutes every hour gives your mind and body a chance to recuperate.

To me this is great news because you get to give yourself a break! Even if being hyperproductive is your goal, you can put in less work and still remain very productive. Yet this idea doesn't always sit well for most high achievers. Despite what science tells us, the need to get everything done at any cost, with the understanding that suffering is necessary to advance, is a problematic belief. Hyperproductivity is the modern-day version of "No pain, no gain."

This perpetually flawed ideology results, time and time again, in physical injury, mental and emotional exhaustion, and strained relationships. Nonetheless, it doesn't stop advertisers and other social influencers from selling this die-hard work "ethic" as a tenet of success. The more you buy into this ideology, the more at risk you are of burning out.

Overtraining Is Burnout

Exercise burnout is a prime example of how broken the "No pain, no gain" philosophy is. Physical overtraining commonly results in strains, sprains, and even severe conditions such as heart disease and asthma. Yet the compulsive need to achieve at any cost gets people back out on the field or in the gym, much sooner than their bodies can handle,

which often results in chronic reinjury and more downtime.

Even when we see the physical effects of overexertion, why do we ignore the signs? Why do we go hard, believing it's the only way to succeed when there is evidence that hyperproductivity actually kills results? The reason is because society's reverence of "hard work" and "climbing to the top" are so ingrained in us that a rare few dare to question it. We're told from a young age that in order to win, we must work hard and be the best—and if there is a chance that someone else may take the lead, then we need to work harder.

TIP

As you read these passages on multitasking, productivity, and performance, notice your automatic response. Do these ideas go against what you believe? Do you understand them on some level, but aren't quite buying it? Do you feel anxious, annoyed, or angry? Or, perhaps you love these ideas and are ready to live this way! Whatever is going on for you right now, simply notice your reactions.

But here's the truth: when you're running a nonstop sprint, you're bound to bonk. As mentioned before, burnout is your signal that the old way of doing things doesn't work; you need to choose differently. Look at it this way: elite and Olympic athletes know the vital importance of not overtraining. With the help of their coaches, they strike a balance of rest and action to maintain optimal focus and function— exerting the right amount of effort (but not overexerting themselves) to produce maximum results. You want to be a top performer, and in order to be your best self, you need to stop overtraining (whether it's in sports, work, or elsewhere). But how?

Mindfulness Is the Way (Out)

Just like peak athletes, top performers in business and other fields know that working smarter, not harder, is the way to uplevel your life. Having interviewed more than two hundred of the world's highest achievers, entrepreneur Tim Ferriss, a notable high achiever himself, affirms that 80 percent of those he spoke to engage in some type of daily meditation or mindfulness practice.

Meditation offers the space to slow down, focus, prioritize, and choose the most effective path. And it's through inner awareness that your mind, body, and emotions can adapt to this new way of relating to yourself, where you no longer need to buy into old, unhelpful patterns of overperforming.

To participate in mindfulness, which is one of many types of meditations, you need to pay attention to a single focal point, such as your breath. This form of meditation has become increasingly popular in the West and is the basis for all awareness practices you'll find in this book. From Buddhist origins, the purpose of mindful meditation was never religious transcendence, but rather a way to train yourself to pay attention. For an added boost, the practice of cultivating gratitude allows your body and mind to pay attention to what's working well in your life. Exercise 6 teaches you an easy way how.

Mindfulness still remains a newer area of research. Even so, with the use of fMRI, EEG, and other medical technologies, mindfulness is shown to change the structure and functioning of the brain. Some of the evidence-based benefits of a mindfulness practice include improved attention, specifically selective attention. This means that instead of having the disorganized brain of a multitasker, you're able to focus on what you want to focus on. It also improves emotional regulation, which lowers the amygdala's fight-flight-freeze mechanism, helping you regain your ability to respond, rather than react, to the world around you. When you practice mindful meditation, you are able to make more conscious choices about how you want to think, feel, and act.

With continued practice, you will gain a new relationship with your mind, body, and emotions. As an active observer, you build the skill of singular focused attention, diminishing the urge to constantly be producing or accomplishing. Turning inward through meditation also teaches you to show up honestly for yourself and helps you see—with crystal clarity—what's truly important to you. You'll be able to make conscious choices about how you want to work, and as you learn to focus and embrace the calm, you'll most likely want to support that sense of well-being by shifting your external behaviors to align with your Inner Knowing.

Exercise 6

BOOSTING GRATITUDE

Objective:
This practice is a little life-hack that helps you feel more appreciative of the good things in your life.

Time + Frequency:
Three minutes; one time daily for at least four weeks.

Directions:

STEP 1: To start, think about something or someone you really appreciate. Create a positive statement about that thing or person with "I get to . . ." and fill in the blank.

Example: "I get to spend Saturday morning with my partner sipping coffee on our couch."

Now you try: "I get to . . .

_____

_____

_____."

STEP 2: Then, be still with this statement and feel a sense of appreciation. Practice this gratitude exercise as often as you want because the more you feel it, the more gratitude will become an ingrained part of your life.

Mindfulness + Productive Rest

Where can this mindfulness practice take you? Living a balanced life does not mean that you will never do something unpleasant ever again. It simply means that when you're guided by your Inner Knowing and your inner flame is lit, you can live with equilibrium and make choices that support your sustainable well-being. You'll be able to set healthy boundaries and connect with people in deeper, more meaningful ways. You'll no longer feel the urge to do everything or be all things to all people—which is impossible anyway and only leads to major burnout.

As with anything new, it will take consistent practice to create this new way of living. In essence, mindfulness is the practice of returning to the present moment. There are different ways to practice mindfulness, but for right now, the important piece is to become aware of what you're doing in the present moment. One way to do this is to focus on your breath, observing as you inhale and exhale. Taking this one step further, you can activate the vagus nerve with a focused breathing technique. The vagus nerve is a large nerve bundle that connects mind and body in a way that triggers the parasympathetic (rest-and-recovery) response in your nervous system.

Gratitude

Drawing from Buddhist principles and scientific results, regular gratitude practice is key to reducing stress and enhancing a sense of fulfillment. But it's difficult to be grateful for much of anything when you're burnt out because your nervous system is already taxed. This is where Exercise 6 *Boosting Gratitude* can support you!

Exercise 7, which will help activate your vagus neve, is not a beginner's practice, but I decided to place it here at the beginning of the book to get you started on your journey and to show you what science has proven is possible. Throughout this book, I offer other proven, practical ways to be mindful in everyday living that will combat burnout and enhance your overall functioning. Try this one out now!

LEARNING TO ACTIVATE YOUR VAGUS NERVE

Objective:

To practice focused breathing in a specific way that counters the physiological effects of burnout by turning on the parasympathetic (rest-and-recovery) mode of your autonomic nervous system.

Time + Frequency:

Five minutes; one time daily for one week (ongoing as needed).

Directions:

To activate the vagus nerve, you'll need to slow your breathing down to five to seven breaths per minute, which equates to twenty seconds per breath. Here, it is broken down into three parts per breath: five count inhale, five count held breath, and ten count exhale (5:5:10).

STEP 1: Sit quietly with your eyes closed and focus your attention on your breath.

STEP 2: Start the breathing sequence *without* the 5:5:10 count as you become acquainted with the rhythm. Do this: inhale, hold, exhale.

STEP 3: Next, with curiosity rather than self-judgment, do your best to breathe in for a count of five, hold for five, and then exhale for ten.

STEP 4: Repeat this breathing rhythm a few more times to the best of your current ability.

STEP 5: Then sit quietly with yourself and notice the thoughts that arise and how your body feels.

STEP 6: Open your eyes to finish this round of the exercise.

Remember, this is an exercise. You're training to reach this slow and conscious breathing pattern—and we're only in the first chapter of the book! Be kind to yourself and know that you won't do it "perfectly" this early on, but you'll get it with practice.

This type of mindfulness practice, what I call "productive rest," teaches your mind and body to value rest. It gives you "something to do" as you learn to choose relaxation and self-awareness over always being productive. Think of it as a weaning-off process, since burnout has resulted in you forgetting how to shut down at the end of the day, or in any moment, in which a bit of rest-and-recovery would be useful. As you begin to settle into productive rest, your restless body calms, your emotions tame, and your mind quiets.

Productive rest creates a feedback loop of communication between the body and mind, reinforcing the benefits of rest. As balance is restored, and you cultivate the beautiful art of "doing nothing" and are able to savor the moment for exactly what your experience is. This whole-system reminder helps you live "in the moment" as you settle into a good book on a Saturday morning or sit poolside and enjoy the feel of the sun on your skin—instead of always feeling on edge, reaching for your phone, or wishing you could relax. Productive rest recharges your energy source, available for when you need to leap into action once again.

Productive rest in everyday practice also teaches you to pace yourself. When you begin, you will feel a strong desire to keep steamrolling through your day, driven by the belief that "faster" and "more" get better results. However, you'll need to suspend this hardwired belief and choose to rest anyway. This is where mini-breaks of productive rest come into play. These mini-breaks of three to fifteen minutes will help you pace yourself and add more mindfulness into everyday living. Before mini-breaks become a habit, you'll need to set reminder alarms, perhaps three per day. When the alarm goes off, stop what you're doing and shift your focus to one thing that is completely different from what you are doing. After three to fifteen minutes of productive rest, you can return to the prior task with a fresher perspective.

Chapter Summary

Being quiet with yourself and being aware of the present moment can feel unsettling and like a waste of time at first. Yet this is the very thing that will lead you out of the exhaustion, anxiousness, and disconnection of burnout and into the productive and meaningful life that you seek. In some ways, it is mind-sets like *I don't have time to rest* or *Resting is a waste of time* that perpetuate our burnout culture . . . and keeps you in it.

We're all susceptible to cultural influences, yet it's your choice of what you want to do with the information you receive—just like it's your choice to do what you will with the information I provide to you. This chapter's goal is to begin debunking some of the cultural myths that keep you burnt out, while also introducing you to the practice of mindfulness and the research that supports healing and sustainable well-being.

Remember, this is your personal healing journey, and this chapter introduced you to the benefits of productive rest. This form of mindfulness offers you tools to connect the mind and body that over time will rewire your internal system so that you can be active and do great things for the rest of your life. From this place of wellness, there's nothing you can't achieve.

Chapter Skill Take-Aways

The exercises in this chapter are designed to reinforce positive healing properties within you.

- *Monotasking* in Exercise 5 counteracts our addiction to multitasking, which helps reduce mental fatigue, increases clarity of thought, and introduces you to very practical aspects of mindfulness. This can be a daily practice done first thing in the morning, such as for two minutes while brushing your teeth, with the potential to extend the practice by choosing to design your day with a task-per-task agenda.

- When you feel burnt out, it can be hard to muster up any form of gratitude—even for the people and things you truly appreciate. *Boosting Gratitude* in Exercise 6 works with your mind and shifts your mood so that you can be more open to the healing properties of gratitude.

- *Learning to Activate Your Vagus Nerve* in Exercise 7 is an advanced breathing practice that begins by simply "starting." Mastery of anything takes time, and when practiced consistently, this skill will reset your nervous system back to rest-and-recovery mode. A key healing component is to allow yourself to be a beginner as you practice with as much self-kindness as you can.

Chapter 2

Body Focus

When you learn to relax your body, your mind begins to relax. This is a golden nugget of truth about burnout prevention and recovery, and it's vital for leading an enlivened life that feels REALLY good. Since we tend to live in a brain-centric world that's focused on intellectual prowess and productivity, we often forget that we even have a body. One of my clients who works in technology described it as "the floating head syndrome." But the act of reclaiming your body as your human powerhouse enables you to rebuild your depleted energy, regain your loss of focus, and learn about the many other ways that burnout uniquely shows up for you. When you're burning out, the symptoms can no longer be ignored, and you must return to your body to restore your health.

Learning about the physiology of burnout earlier in this book, you now know that your nervous system is in "survival mode" when you feel stressed and overwhelmed. However, this isn't a comfortable or sustainable way for your body to function—and it leaves you feeling like you want to escape, jump to the next task, or do anything to feel better.

In this state, there's a feedback message surging through your whole system that signals, *I can't relax.* You feel anxious and like you need to fill your free time with an activity. This internal drive to push harder is both initiated and perpetuated by your body's current inability to feel calm and rested. Once you retrain your body to rest, you can truly be with yourself and you'll be more open and available for yourself and your life's responsibilities. Clarity, creativity, and innovation can emerge from this space of calm well-being, and it also uncovers your lost sense of "self"—that person who's fun, loving, playful, interesting, and able to sustain deeply meaningful and connected relationships.

By working with your body, you will strengthen your ability to relax and feel safe, as each state plays off the other. You will move from survival mode, the sensed lack of safety and distress, to thrival mode, the deep sense of safety that relaxes and enlivens you. As you enhance your body awareness practice to de-stress in this chapter, you are honing your skills to step into a felt sense of what I call "Grounded Expansion."

Grounded Expansion

Grounded Expansion is the ability to feel deeply connected to yourself through the physical body (being grounded), and it's from this strong foundation that you're able to safely challenge yourself to open up and thrive (expansion). In this state, you're safe, confident, and able to evolve into the person you are meant to be. Burnout shows up as "ungrounded constriction" that misplaces your sense of personal empowerment and sends you on a temporary detour. The practice toward Grounded Expansion through your physical body will awaken you to endless possibilities—not endless overwhelm—as you learn to let your body take the lead. Exercise 8 gives you the chance to begin feeling Grounded Expansion for yourself.

As long as you're alive, your mind will never stop functioning, but it doesn't need to be on "high alert" or "overthinking" all of the time. There's plenty of room to let your body take the lead sometimes. Learning to reground into your body on a daily basis has multiple benefits, which will continue to be explored throughout the following chapters. Quite literally, placing focus on your body reminds your mind that you're a physical being, which in turn helps lower cortisol and

GROUNDED EXPANSION

Objective:

This exercise is a way to accept your body as a place of strength, rooted like a tree, to provide the basis of feeling confident, alive, and ready to be fully you.

Time + Frequency:

Five minutes; three times per week for a minimum of two weeks (ongoing as needed).

Directions:

STEP 1: Begin by standing with your feet at a comfortable distance apart. With your eyes open, look at your body (standing in front of a full-length mirror is recommended). Look at yourself standing, while you feel your feet planted firmly on the floor. Now feel your feet grounded into the earth, as if they are roots of a tree.

STEP 2: Close your eyes and continue to notice the feeling of your feet rooted into the ground.

STEP 3: From here, stand as tall as possible, without forcing it. Standing tall and rooted, raise your arms out to your sides, extending up at an angle in a "V" formation toward the sky. Remaining as grounded as possible in your feet and lower body, allow for the sense of extension upward though your arms and out your fingertips as if they are tree limbs reaching for the warm sun. Relaxing your shoulders, breathe as you normally would.

STEP 4: Remain here for one to three minutes as you simultaneously feel the anchor of your foothold and your capacity for expansion through your arms and fingertips. When your mind wanders, return its focus to your body's current action.

STEP 5: Once complete, release your arms from this position and place one hand on your heart and one on your belly. With eyes closed, notice how both your body and your mind feel in the moment. Then open your eyes, notice your body in the mirror, and return to your day.

other stress hormone levels to reduce the physical feeling of being on edge and "always on."

As you grow an intimate and loving relationship with your body, you'll gain the ability to feel safe wherever you are. This is super helpful, given that environmental factors add to your stress level and can get you off track. So much of how and why you choose to move through the world is seeking external validation. Although this isn't necessarily a bad thing, when you rely too heavily on outside markers that define how to live and attain success, you can spend your whole life trying to prove yourself. This is exhausting and places you at high risk of burnout.

Let's take a moment to consider some of the reasons we seek validation: we want to feel worthy, safe, whole, and free. These are understandable human desires and are even components of optimal wellness. Yet when you're driven primarily by outside sources, your ability to naturally heal is hindered. What other people think of you, what your work accomplishments are, how much money you have, whether you're in a relationship or not, and other social markers of success can place so much pressure on you that you work too hard to accomplish these goals, resulting in burnout.

Of course, it's normal and healthy for you to want to be liked and respected, do excellent work, have financial security or abundance, and be in a healthy, loving relationship. But you have to feel worthy, safe, whole, and free within yourself before anything else—and the first step is to get out of your head and in touch with your body. As you deepen your true connection to self, the more you'll be able to truly connect with others and use your own power when challenges arise to strengthen your inner resolve.

Create Readiness for Change

Change is inevitable. Take the human body, for example. Your hair grows at an average rate of 0.35 mm per day, your red blood cells are replaced every 120 days, and your entire skeleton is replaced every ten years (10 percent per year). Not only is your body changing, but it's regenerating and must perform the ongoing cycles of life and death in order to remain in homeostasis, which is the body's drive to maintain internal stability.

We are thinking and feeling beings, which means our survival instinct registers "change" as something unknown, with a potentially dangerous outcome. This is because, along with our body's wisdom to trust and "go with the flow," we're hardwired to fear change, and when burnout resides in the body, we're always in survival mode.

The truth is that it's human to want to grow, change, and evolve—but when the two mechanisms of "growth" and "fear of change" are in opposition to each other, internal conflict and stress will keep you feeling stuck. As you begin to loosen the reins of your brain-centric ways and ground into your body, change will start to feel more natural and more manageable.

Beyond your automatic internal workings, conscious choice comes into play, allowing you to decide to do things differently. The process of deciding to change tends to be gradual and occurs at a tipping point when the pain of how you're currently living becomes too painful to bear—leaving you with no other choice *but* to change. In my observation of working with people who experience burnout, the comfort zone of living with this discomfort slows their decision to recognize they need help. The other side of burnout can feel so scary and unknown that your conscious psyche rejects the idea of change and real help and relief are often delayed.

The fear of change can show up as convincing yourself that change is impossible, or that you feel too stuck to do anything about your burnout. However, acknowledging the fear and choosing to change anyway sets the process of fear reduction in motion as you prove to yourself that transforming is not a life-or-death situation. When you can begin to understand what is holding you back, you can then consciously and courageously choose change. Taking small steps, while grounding into the healing presence of your body, helps release the fear of change as you proceed on your healing path.

The truth is, committing to heal from burnout means committing to change. The fact that you have picked up this book tells me that you've already faced some resistance to change and are ready for something different. You don't want to be burnt out—nor do you want to live in your current state forever. As you move through this change process, optimal wellness will become your new reality.

Keep in mind (and body) that the healing process is nonlinear. At times you may feel like you're rapidly evolving and other times you may feel like you're stuck in molasses, and there will likely be times when you feel like you're going backward. I know this can feel frustrating, but it's part of how real change works, by teaching you to create a new pace and become more comfortable with change.

Although the urge to quit is quite normal, I want you to stick with it. I don't want your survival instinct to kick in and have you exit partway through the process. By tuning in to your body's ability to ground you, you will learn to feel safe and protected in the midst of change. This will help you fight the urge to return to the comforts of the familiar, yet unhealthy "discomfort" you know so well.

When you're ready to move through a new kind of discomfort that will result in greater long-term ease and life fulfillment, your body will lead the way. Currently you know what burnout feels like for you, but you don't know what the other side of burnout is yet. This unknown can feel destabilizing, and I bet you want to know what your future life will look and feel like. So, let's take a moment now to practice and visualize how wellness feels in your body in Exercise 9.

This exercise is to be done *now* (don't skip it!). My reason for urging you to do it now is that anything new can be easily pushed off until later. By showing up for yourself today, and every day, with the intention to heal from burnout, you're moving at *your* natural pace of healing. By allowing your body to be your guide, your resistance to change will begin to lessen. As you become more comfortable with change through this recovery process, you'll become more prepared to take on new challenges with lesser feelings of stress.

TIP

Do your best to not force any of these body-awareness practices or to judge yourself on how "good" (or "bad") you're doing them. Since we're socially trained to pay attention to our intellect and pretty much ignore our bodies, it will take some practice to efficiently sense your body.

BODY-AWARENESS MEDITATION

Objective:

You're gaining rudimentary skills on how to pay attention to your body and tune in to its safety and feel-good potential.

Time + Frequency:

Five minutes; three times per week for a minimum of two weeks (ongoing as needed).

Directions:

In preparation, choose a three-word mantra (use the one you created in Exercise 4 *Three-Word Mantra* on page 20).

STEP 1: Begin seated in a chair and close your eyes. Say to yourself, *I'm aware that I'm sitting in a chair.* Repeat this phrase while you notice your whole body sitting in the chair. Once your inner awareness has focused on your body in the chair, stay with this focus for two breaths.

STEP 2: Then add your chosen three-word mantra:

"I choose _____."

As you sit in this position with your attention turned inward, repeat this wellness mantra and sense how your body responds. Stay with this whole-body sense of wellness as you repeat the healing mantra at least five times.

STEP 3: Release the mantra and be with the feeling in your body for a few more breaths. Notice how the sensations within your body may have shifted from when you first sat down to do the exercise. Slowly open your eyes when ready.

Achieving a Mindful Body

Your body functions in the present moment—without judgment. It accepts and responds to whatever is happening in real time. This is why your body is one of your greatest teachers to hone present moment awareness, since it's ever-changing as the new present moment arrives and is willing to receive a new experience.

Although your body is always in the present moment, it's not separate from your mind and holds on to old patterns, stuck stress, and traumatic memories of past experiences. It still remains in the present, observing and receptive to the here and now.

Whether your thoughts are in the past, present, or future, your body responds to them as if they're in the present moment. Your physical self doesn't know the difference between the thought of eating ice cream and actually eating ice cream. The more you can align your thoughts with actual events, the more connected you'll be with your body's present moment awareness.

Your body is like a living, breathing time capsule that stores significant memories. And your mind is a time machine that toggles between the past and the future, rarely stopping in the present. The more you can teach your time-traveling mind to stay in the present, the more in sync your body and mind will become. When both are focused on the present moment, the illusion of "separateness" dissolves and they function as one.

When you're no longer bombarded by the stress induced by the time-traveling mind, your body and mind are truly integrated. Your whole system becomes less muddled by past conditions and future concerns, and a profound new level of clarity emerges for both body and mind. This translates to more ease, self-trust, flexibility, agility, willingness to change, flow, and the ability to move through the world in a whole new way. Balance is restored and healing can take place on deeper levels.

The communication between body and mind is interactive and goes both ways, meaning that the body responds to the mind, just as the mind responds to the messages of the body. To practice present moment awareness that aligns these two areas, you can start with either your mind or your body. If you want to start with your mind, use your cognitive awareness to focus directly on what actions your body is doing in the present moment. For example, if you're eating an ice cream cone, focus on the experience: notice how you hold the cone, how you lick it, what it tastes like, what it looks like. This practice allows you to be with your body by engaging your mind with the actions of the present moment.

If you want to start by shifting focus to your body itself—not on the external observations, but rather on your body's existence—keep with the ice cream example used above and pay attention to how your body is receiving it. Does it feel cold on your throat as you're eating, are you getting a brain freeze, are you experiencing a slight sugar rush? More examples of this body response approach include paying attention to your breath, placing your hand to your heart and feeling it beat, and feeling the sensation of your skin against the air.

There are many body-based practices that can attune your mind to present moment awareness—and there's no "perfect" way—so I urge you to come up with a few of your own that feel right to you. The more you explore and learn how you can return to your body's present moment awareness, the brighter your innate wisdom will shine as your physicality takes the lead.

Acquainting the Body + Mind Every Day

The idea of aligning your body and mind through daily mindfulness practices can seem like an abstract concept at first. But the HtBR (Head to Body Ratio) is a tool that can help you pay attention to your body and mind by making mindfulness a user-friendly, daily practice. The HtBR is a way to remind yourself to pay attention to your body and mind by asking yourself, *How much of me is living in my head, and how much of me is living in my body, right now?* It is set up as a fraction with the numerator being your head, or your thinking brain, and the denominator being your body. For example, if you find that most of your awareness is in your thoughts (your head), which is very common, then a likely numerator would be eighty, and the denominator would be twenty (both numbers need to add up to one hundred). See below for a visual of an HtBR of 80/20:

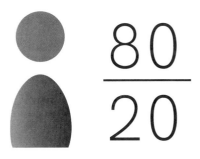

This may still seem very abstract, and at first you may have some trouble understanding how to feel into your body. This is normal AND a big reason why I suggest you begin using this tool. With a bit of practice, the answer to your current HtBR will start to come more easily to you.

This isn't a mathematical equation, and therefore there is no perfect answer and there's no way to do it wrong. You cannot plug these numbers into a formula to calculate "how burnt out I am." It's simply an awareness tool—a way to check in with your body and mind on a daily basis as you form the new habit of body-mind integration. Let's try it now in Exercise 10.

Exercise 10

DETERMINING YOUR HtBR

Objective:

This is a quick tool to get you acquainted with your body in relation to your mind to use at any time throughout your day. It's great for beginners to build awareness around body-mind connection, or it can be an advanced practice once you learn to determine your HtBR in seconds.

Time + Frequency:

Under one minute; three times per day for at least one month (or until it becomes a habit).

Directions:

STEP 1: Sit quietly for a few moments (eyes can be open or closed) and ask yourself, *How much of me is living in my head, and how much of me is living in my body, right now?*

STEP 2: Remain in quiet observance as the numerator and denominator come to you.

STEP 3: Jot down the equation (either in your mind's eye, your phone, or on a piece of paper).

"My current HtBR is . . . "

The answer may come to you right away, especially after the first few tries, or it may take longer than you expect to tune into your HtBR. Just try not to overthink it and be patient with yourself. This is totally new to you, and new things take time to learn and get used to.

Through working with clients, I developed this tool to build "on-the-go" self-awareness. And it has proven to be extremely effective in teaching people how to do quick body-mind check-ins on a daily basis, anytime and anywhere. HtBR can be completed in less than a minute, and with some practice, you'll be able to make the assessment in less than twenty seconds.

This exercise will help you learn to quickly attune to your body-mind. With that being said, speed isn't always the goal when it comes to recovering from burnout. Yet, given that you live and work in a fast-paced world, this quick tool will serve you well throughout the day. I recommend that you practice HtBR at least three times a day. Try starting when you first wake up in a quiet space of your home, and then do it two more times during the day when you're engaged in daily living.

If you had only one tool in your burnout-recovery tool kit, I would recommend HtBR. By checking in with yourself in this simple way, you are creating new habits: you're learning to give yourself a break. You're allowing your body to take the lead.

You're teaching the mind to STOP what it's doing, if only for twenty seconds to a minute. This is more powerful than it may seem. When you make a conscious decision to shift your perspective from being on autopilot for your daily habits, you break the cycle of pushing yourself through to the end of the day—a frantic way of life that perpetuates burnout.

By choosing to use the HtBR tool, you're seamlessly infusing rest-and-recovery into your otherwise stressful day. And since actions done over time have a cumulative effect, these mini-breaks of body-mind awareness will make you feel more at ease and capable of meeting your daily demands.

As I've seen with my clients, HtBR is one of the single most effective tools of transformation. This simple technique has the power to shift your awareness to create fluid communication between your body and mind. In time, you'll see how showing up for yourself in this new way can reshape your concept of who you are and how you move through the world.

Celebrate the Gradual Process of Change

At the start of my healing process from depression, which primarily showed up as debilitating self-doubt and very low self-esteem, I learned to celebrate the small wins. Even a glint of hope, a genuine laugh, or a few moments of an uplifted mood were enough to celebrate. I carry this gift of healing with me as I continue to celebrate and acknowledge the joys of living. I share this insight with my clients, and now I'm sharing it with you.

The more I paid attention to the good around me, the more I gained a sense of empowerment in knowing that healing is possible. It taught me to appreciate the healing journey and experience the full scope of my recovery. In time, I realized that there were more celebrated moments—and they stuck around longer—and soon my depression disappeared.

When you're used to being one way for so long, especially if you find yourself in a dark place, any glimpse of light can easily be missed, ignored, or downplayed. This can stunt the healing process and make it much harder on you. Yet, when you shift your focus to the possibility of change and become aware of the present moment, your odds of feeling better increase—and you can recognize and celebrate those little moments of ease, joy, and true connection.

Celebrate

Pausing and spending a few moments acknowledging your experience and celebrating it has many healing benefits. You can celebrate the experience in any way you choose, but the important thing is to really mean it and feel it. This may be difficult at first, so try imagining that you're celebrating a friend's accomplishments. For example, if you choose to celebrate with a positive statement like "Way to go!," say this to yourself like you would say it to a close friend. Feel the excitement, pride, and celebratory vibe in your body.

As you move along this healing path, there may be big moments of sudden transformation. Yet, most of the time, progress will be gradual; you may even find yourself feeling frustrated by the pace and start to doubt yourself or get stuck on the idea that you'll always be stuck. But celebrating the small wins not only gives you hope, but it also reinforces those moments as real. With purposeful intention, more of these moments will occur, opening you up to an easier way of being.

The other thing that can happen if you don't cultivate an awareness practice that celebrates small victories is that you may not recognize how far you've come. This can place you at risk for relapse because when life brings new and additional stressors, which it will, you may be more critical of yourself for not being able to handle them better and spiral back into burnout.

The practice of self-awareness, kindness, and gratitude is a huge aspect of burnout recovery, because it helps bring you to a place of sustainable well-being. In your recovery from burnout, I not only urge you to learn to sense into the ways burnout shows up in your body, but also notice when your body is feeling more relaxed. Ease into that feeling as well and celebrate it. Even if it's fleeting, acknowledge and appreciate those few moments when you feel solid, safe, and more like yourself. The practice of feeling more peaceful and revitalized is a process that takes time, dedication, and a willingness to show up.

Body Awareness

Identifying distress in your body is a useful way to learn how to de-stress and gain more energy. Muscle tension and held breath are two major signposts of "stuck stress" that make life harder and create unnecessary fatigue. In essence, the harder you try, the harder life becomes. This may not seem true since it has been socially ingrained in us that we must work hard to excel—and if things aren't working out as planned, then the answer is to push harder. Does this ring true for you? We must first learn how to recognize stress in our bodies.

Recognizing Tension

Tension becomes evident in the different ways that you habitually use your body. How you carry yourself (your posture and automatic ways of doing daily actions) likely expends more energy than you realize. Since your body and mind respond to one another, the belief system that says you need to "produce, do more, and be more" shows up in your body as tension, which is "stuck stress." You burn out because of the tendency to work beyond the hours you need to and strive to be as productive as humanly possible. But when is it time to call it a day? When have you done enough? When is it time to pivot? When is it time to course correct? And most importantly, when will you surrender your mind's need to *always* be in control and let your body take the lead?

Muscle tension and constriction is a strong physical cue that you're working harder than you need to for the results you desire. Learning to pay attention to how you use your body is not only a useful body-based awareness practice to strengthen body-mind coherency, but it can also teach you how working harder is oftentimes less efficient than reducing the pressure and letting go. This helps reinforce a new mind-set that doing less allows you to get more done. You'll soon gain the tools to build awareness and loosen the tension in your body so that you'll not only feel better physically but also experience a new level of vitality that will help you get more done with ease.

Let's first look at some small, mundane habits in your life that are opportunities to facilitate major change. I'll share a personal example. Every morning, I would make a green smoothie with frozen mango chunks. Like clockwork, I'd open the freezer, take out the bag of mango, and remove the elastic band that held it closed. One morning, after at least a year of making these daily smoothies, I paid attention to how I opened the bag. My shoulders were scrunched up toward my ears, my arms were tensed, and my

fingers were working the elastic of the bag as if I were opening a lockbox with the wrong key.

In that moment of awareness, I realized I was wrangling an elastic band off a plastic bag as if my life depended on it. I also realized that this was an opportunity to release myself from the unnecessary tension I had patterned myself into. So, I chose to do it differently. I stopped what I was doing, took a full deep breath, loosened the tension in my shoulders, and consciously removed the elastic with very little effort. My shoulders immediately relaxed, and my body felt less tense. I realized I was making this morning task harder than it needed to be simply because it had become my body's way of doing it.

Off the top of your head, think of some ways you may be holding your posture and creating unnecessary muscle tension. Perhaps you're tightening your jaw, scrunching your

> **TIP**
>
> In some very concrete ways, we work harder than we need to, which results in a lowered Return on Investment (ROI) and depletes our energy unnecessarily. Noticing how we hold tension in our body gives us the opportunity to release the extra effort and practice doing less for better results.

shoulders up toward your ears, or constricting your belly. Habitually held muscle tension can also show up as headaches, stomachaches, and unexplained aches and pains. It takes awareness and practice to undo our old unhelpful habits. But as you start paying attention to how you hold yourself, you'll be able to release yourself from stuck stress. Let's start by practicing a tool for tension awareness and release called *Freeze Frame Awareness* in Exercise 11.

Recognizing Breathing

Breath matters. Held and shallow breathing often accompany your body's tense actions and keep you feeling more stuck and closed off. When you remember to breathe and deepen your breath, it helps release muscle tension and naturally self-soothes by triggering your body's relaxation response (the parasympathetic nervous system). It also creates space where there seemingly wasn't any before. In quantum terms, human beings are comprised of more than 99.99999999999 percent space. Breath helps you access and allow for more of that space to be sensed. By enabling efficient delivery of oxygen to your cells, you'll feel more energized and lighter mentally, emotionally, and physically. Since the first step is always awareness, take note of your breath right now. Notice whether it's being held or whether it is shallow in your

Exercise 11

FREEZE FRAME AWARENESS

Objective:

Like a snapshot in time, this exercise is designed to build your awareness of feeling your body in positions that compromise your health.

Time + Frequency:

Two minutes; one time daily as you build awareness of your held tension with opportunity to release it (ongoing as needed).

Directions:

STEP 1: When a moment occurs that you're gripping or holding something, take pause.

STEP 2: Notice your held muscle tension without self-judgment.

STEP 3: Breathe into the tensed area, and on the exhale, explore how you can release this extra effort (i.e., relax your shoulders to where they normally rest).

STEP 4: Slowly breathe in and out of the area you just released for at least five breaths.

STEP 5: Sit quietly and simply notice how you feel.

upper chest, as this is an opportunity to take in oxygen differently.

Body-focused breathing, a technique shared in Exercise 12, brings muscle tension and breath awareness together to help you de-stress and reenergize.

As with all the provided exercises, do your best not to force the action or judge yourself. If you're having difficulty feeling into your body or taking fuller breaths, or if you're not feeling relaxed right away, it's okay. The stuck stress didn't happen overnight, so it may take some time to feel it. Similarly, the constriction of shallow breathing means it will take time to expand. Repeated practice of these and the other tools will help you retrain your body-mind to feel relaxed. For now, stick with it, be kind to yourself, and as the awareness builds, the more you will feel!

As you strengthen your muscle tension release and breath awareness practices, you may even start to notice your tendency to hold more tension in specific arenas of your life. For example, I'm not big on cooking and have found that I carry my body in more tense ways while doing activities in the kitchen. I'll clench my jaw when I am sautéing at the stovetop, or, as you read from my earlier mango smoothie story, I'd scrunch my shoulders when I open frozen mango bags. For many people, cooking is more of a meditative act; the kitchen is where they feel most relaxed and at ease. What causes stress or tension varies from person to person, so begin to notice not only how you hold tension, but also

Exercise 12

BODY-FOCUSED BREATHING

Objective:

As an extension of Exercise 11, *Freeze Frame Awareness* (see page 57), this exercise will enhance your ability to locate tension in your body. Through conscious use of your breath, you'll become increasingly aware of how the tension shows up, as well as your ability to release it.

Time + Frequency:

Three minutes; five times per week for two weeks (ongoing as needed).

Directions:

STEP 1: With your eyes closed, scan your body and notice where your body is holding tension.

STEP 2: Inhale into the area of tension and exhale out.

STEP 3: Remaining focused on the specific area of tension in your body, repeat this a few more times (at least five, and upward to as many as you'd like). Notice how your body feels and how your posture may have shifted.

in what contexts. This will help you become extra mindful during activities that push your stress button.

So often we muscle through life—tense and exhausted, as we muscle unconsciously through the motions. If you continue to force, push, and make things happen at any cost, then you're simply working too hard and you'll crash and burn. With awareness and practice, your life will become less about struggle and more about finesse. Think of it as moving "from force to finesse," which is the utilization of the body in more energy-efficient ways to decrease stress and enhance overall well-being. The key is to notice, breathe, and release as you take steps forward with more easeful action. Exercise 13 is another great tool to propel you in this direction.

Your Burnout Metaphor

By now, you know that burnout constricts your body, and you're learning how to move out of that reality into one that feels more fluid and easeful. You're beginning to pay attention to how you (within your body) maneuver through your day and how you can make conscious choices to hold your body differently to release the "stuck stress." As mentioned earlier, burnout is the accumulated result of ongoing and chronic stress that cuts off clear communication between your

What Is Shallow Breathing?

In short, shallow breathing occurs when you breathe in and out of your upper chest, placing strain on your throat muscles to pass the air in and out of your body. This form of breathing becomes habitual for most people under stress, which can induce hyperventilation and increase anxious feelings. As a shallow breather learns to deepen their breath by using more of the lungs' full capacity, overall respiratory health improves, and so does the ability to calm the physiological responses of stress and anxiety.

body and mind, manifesting differently for each person who suffers from it. This means that your lived experience of burnout is unique to you and healing from it will be too.

Fully understanding your lived experience of burnout within your body can be challenging in two ways: (1) because it has been your norm for so long, you may not realize there is another way, and (2) you may not have a language for it. When you don't

BREATHING SLOWER

Objective:

Breathing slower builds your capacity to breathe deeper with more ease. As you move out of the habit of shallow breathing, this exercise will help you gradually open your lungs to a fuller capacity so you can breathe deeply.

Time + Frequency:

Five minutes; three times per week for two weeks (ongoing as needed).

Directions:

STEP 1: Begin seated with your eyes closed and notice your breath. Don't try to change your breathing pattern in any way; observe without judgment.

STEP 2: After you've followed your inhalation and exhalation for a few rounds, count the inhale from start to finish. Then count the exhale from start to finish. This will give you a number to work with, such as "three counts in and four counts out."

STEP 3: Now, continue breathing in and out to that same count, and begin to slow your count down. You'll still inhale to that same count of three and exhale to the same count of four, but your count between each number will become longer to slow your breathing down. Complete at least ten rounds of this slowed breathing exercise.

STEP 4: To finish, release the count, breathe as your body naturally does, and spend a few moments noticing how your body feels. This exercise will be tricky at first, but with a bit of practice, you'll you get the hang of it.

have words to describe how things are, the use of metaphor can play an important role in expressing what's happening for you. And, in turn, it can help facilitate the undoing and release of the unwanted experience. A metaphor is a figure of speech that is not literal in its representation yet is symbolic and can provide a different way to explain something that feels abstract, like burnout. This concept of describing your experience of burnout through metaphor and then releasing it will become clearer when you practice it. So, let's jump right in with Exercise 14 to create your own burnout metaphor.

Your Body as a Safe Base

Think of your body as a secure base—the place you can return to when life feels chaotic and out of control. Threads of this concept are derived from attachment theory of developmental psychology. According to attachment theory, a child's connection to their primary caregiver (usually the mother) determines how safe they feel about the world. As a child, the safer you felt and more trusting you were of your caregiver's ability to meet your needs, the more open you were to explore the world, knowing you could go back to the safe base of your caregiver at any time.

A less secure attachment results in a sense of inner chaos and a feeling that the world is unreliable and unsafe. In this case, you'd explore less, be less creative, and take fewer risks.

With a secure attachment to your own body, you can safely and confidently explore the world around you. You can be creative, take risks, make mistakes, grow, change, and evolve. You can move

The Physical Benefits of Visualization

Remember how you learned earlier in this chapter that the body is responding to the mind in real time, whether that scenario is actually happening or it's just an idea? The fact is, your body believes what your mind tells it. Further, your subconscious mind processes information through imagery and symbolism. Therefore, visualization techniques help merge your mind and body into an effective tool for transformation, helping you reveal your deeper experiences of burnout in order to undo it.

CREATE YOUR OWN BURNOUT
METAPHOR AND RELEASE STRATEGY

Objective:

The premise of this practice is to get in touch with the deeper visceral levels of your burnout through the use of metaphor in Part 1. You will then practice visually undoing burnout within your body and mind to release yourself from the confines of "stuck stress" in Part 2. I recommend doing this practice daily for at least a week and observe how your body, mind, mood, and energy levels shift. There's no way to mess up this exercise. It's an act of exploring how your mind and body can help each other communicate abstract sensation in ways to lessen stress and enhance well-being.

Time + Frequency:

Initial setup time of Part 1 is five to ten minutes; Part 2 is five to ten minutes; after doing the full exercise once, practice Part 2 daily for one week (repeat as needed).

Directions:

The first part is to identify an appropriate metaphor for your burnout, and the second is to create a guided meditation that visually "undoes" the imagery of stuckness so you can learn to let go of stress. Be creative and get curious.

Part 1:
Identify Your Burnout Metaphor

STEP 1: Think about how you would metaphorically describe your burnout by tuning in to your body to feel your visceral experience of burnout. For help, review the examples provided. Then see which metaphor resonates with your experience. Once chosen, write down your burnout metaphor.

Examples of burnout metaphors:

- White-knuckling it through life

- Working my way into a corner that I need to get myself out of

- Feeling like I'm getting pulled in different directions at 100 mph

- A drained battery than can no longer hold a charge

- A long, dark tunnel with seemingly no end

- Being on a hamster wheel that self-propels ever faster

Create your own:

Part 2:
Visualize Your Burnout Metaphor to Get Unstuck

STEP 1: Begin seated or standing (whatever makes the most sense, given your metaphor) and close your eyes.

STEP 2: Spend a few moments getting grounded within your body. (If it helps, you could say, *I'm aware that I am sitting/ standing right now.*)

STEP 3: Then bring your burnout metaphor into your mind's eye and envision yourself experiencing it. As an example, feel the tension and terror of "white-knuckling it through life," in both your body and mind.

STEP 4: Now, begin to allow the constraints of the metaphor to loosen as you visualize its release. Continuing with the "white-knuckling" example, imagine the engine slowing down as it releases the visceral grip of your burnout experience. You will start to feel lighter; you can breathe slower and fuller.

STEP 5: To finish the exercise, remain quiet and still. Notice how your internal sense of burnout may have shifted.

forward with self-assurance and ease. When things begin to feel chaotic, disorganized, or risky, you know you can always return focus to your body because it's from that secure base that you feel safe; you can regroup and head back out into the world to try again.

At the start of burnout recovery, your body doesn't feel like a safe place you can return to. This is for two main reasons: (1) having spent much of your adult life in your head, you're just now cultivating a true relationship with your body, and like all relationships, it will take some time to grow a trusting friendship. And, (2) the physical symptoms of burnout, including the hijacked nervous system responses, tensions, and other aches and pains, don't send a message to your mind that your body can be trusted.

Yet, it is to be trusted, and with time and practice, you'll know this within yourself. Once the symptoms of burnout begin to subside, you will begin to see that your body isn't a nuisance, a side thought, or a place that holds all your discomfort. Through this healing process, your body will become your biggest comfort in a changing world.

So much of our stress comes from not having all the answers—not being able to control what's going to happen. Whether it's uncertainty at work or in your personal life, it's impossible to predict your future.

For many people, this is a very destabilizing concept, so we try our best to control as much of our lives as we possibly can. Yet, control is ultimately an illusion, and as you learn to surrender to this fact, the more open you will become to the joy of living with less stress, worry, and the need for control. Even the idea of this might have you feeling a bit scared right now, which is a very normal human reaction. Remember, your body holds the key to releasing this fear by returning yourself to the sense of safety that resides within you.

We live in the age of digital too much information (TMI): access to information is available 24/7, ever increasing in quantity and speed of accessibility. We're bombarded every day with information overload, often with conflicting messaging. This can easily have you second-guessing what you know, what you want to do, and who you are—leaving you with a stress-inducing conundrum. Yet, there's an antidote to fear and anxiety: trust yourself. By learning to re-ground into your body's sense of safety, you can calm down and get to know who you really are. You will become confident and know what the right next step is for you.

Since your body is literally with you everywhere you go, you can re-ground in the present moment, anytime and anywhere. How convenient is that? In the exact moment that you start to feel uncomfortable, you can return to your body for reassurance and then go on with your day. This practice of surrendering to the present moment and choosing your body as the focal point helps you heal from burnout, while deepening your internal sense of "knowing"—a life skill that will serve you well.

From Book Knowledge to Embodied "Knowing"

Have you ever had the experience of learning something and then having that new information develop into a deeper sense of knowing, as if you could "feel it in your bones"? Up until this point in life, you may have accepted your reality as truth, since your intellectual and rational self understood the ideology, yet lacked sensory depth. This heady experience can be rather surfacey, and when it comes to wellness concepts it can feel difficult to fully integrate for real change. The longer you know, believe, and live these concepts within your body and mind, the more your life circumstances and experiences become "cellular memory." This is how consistency and a willingness to show up for yourself truly builds a healing lifestyle based on inner trust and embodied knowing.

Cellular Memory

Your entire body—all the way down to the cellular level—is listening to your mind's instructions. When the message is stress-related, your cells remember how to be stressed. The more you think and feel a certain way, the more your cellular memory aligns with this way of being. The good news is you can create new cellular memory by taking in new information and practicing it until it becomes your new way. We're very good at intellectualizing what we know because we spend a disproportionate amount of time in our heads. This is not a negative thing in and of itself, but it can hinder your capacity to know something on a deeper level—which is where true healing happens. To heal from burnout, you must experience this book for yourself so that it becomes a real and meaningful personal experience.

As you strengthen your Inner Knowing while working with this book, you may at times find yourself outright rejecting a certain idea or practice. It is absolutely your right to do so, but if it feels like a knee-jerk reaction, I suggest you consider the reasoning behind it. Feelings and thoughts of strong objection can arise for two main reasons: (1) the concept truly doesn't align with who you are, and therefore it's not your truth, and (2) it hit a nerve because on some level you're sensing it to be true—yet, this new truth scares you because you are forced to question old belief systems. This means you will have to change some of your old ways to overcome burnout, and that can feel terrifying.

As you move through this book, you'll learn new ways to show up honestly for yourself. So, read on with an open mind and an open heart. Allow the ideas to enter your head and sense the information with your body. Practice the exercises and self-reflect on your experiences. Keep what is true, and simply let go of the rest.

Chapter Summary

In this chapter, you learned why your body is so vital to burnout recovery as well as practical ways to be in your body more often. Body-based awareness is a recurring theme throughout this entire book because the body is at the foundation of all healing, but it's often ignored. As you learn how to release the tension, the holding, and the extra "efforting" that's just unnecessary, you begin to settle into ease and grace. From the safe base of your body, you will witness the true strength of who you are.

Healing is not a linear path, and real change has its challenges. The key is to always return to your body so that you don't overexert or avoid the tough stuff. Listen to your body because it will tell you when to rest, when to act, and when to change course. It will teach you how not to overdo it and find a balanced internal state. You are enough. You do enough. There's nothing to prove. You are learning to fully trust yourself and move forward in life from a grounded sense of expansion.

Feel the ground underneath your feet as you stand with confidence. Your body is strong, yet buoyant. From this place of self-empowerment, you're exactly where you need to be, and all is possible. We still have much more to explore, as we delve deeper into the mind in the next chapter and then emotions after that. But what you've learned thus far and will continue to practice is setting you up for success in both resolving burnout and stepping into thrive mode.

Chapter Skill Take-Aways

You must practice new ways of doing things—within both your body and your mind—in order to create actual change. Here's a review of the exercises you've been practicing, along with suggestions on how to move forward with them throughout this book and as part of your continuing wellness exploration:

- Exercise 8 *Grounded Expansion* and Exercise 9 *Body-Awareness Meditation* are both active tools to get you feeling solid in your body as you extend yourself into a deeper sense of wellness. Your potential is unlimited, and these exercises serve as reminders of this sustainable truth that will become your cellular memory.

- Exercise 10 *Determining Your HtBR* is an ideal daily practice—a quick way to remind yourself within a given day that you have a body. This helps connect your body and mind as one whole working system for coherent clarity of thoughts, emotions, and actions.

- Through Exercise 11 *Freeze Frame Awareness* and Exercise 12 *Body-Focused Breathing*, you learn to embody the knowledge that "more isn't always better," and you recognize that letting go of the unnecessary tension lessens your ingrained need for "excess efforting" that can lead to exhaustion. With Exercise 13 *Breathing Slower*, you deepen your capacity to be with yourself in honest ways that support healing and longevity with more grace and ease.

- When you *Create Your Own Burnout Metaphor and Release Strategy* in Exercise 14, you not only gain awareness of how you feel on subconscious levels, but you also teach your body and mind the valuable lesson of self-healing; since all parts of you work together, you feel better. As mentioned in the exercise instructions, I recommend that you practice this daily for one week. After that, you can continue to practice it, return to it at a later point in time, or create another metaphor when you're faced with a major life challenge.

Chapter 3

Mind Focus

We identify with what we're thinking so closely that "what we think" seems to be "who we are." Our thoughts seem solid, tangible, and therefore absolutely true. Thoughts are powerful because we attach them to our belief systems. Yet, a belief is simply a thought that has been repeated enough times that it becomes the truth. Your willingness to think or believe differently releases the hold, and therefore the power. It's your choice to change your mind—and your willingness to do so is the basis behind a growth mind-set and the ability to heal from burnout.

Awareness of your thoughts is *absolutely necessary* for change. This is no small task since much of what you think about over the course of a day goes unrealized because: (1) much of what you think lies below the surface in your subconscious mind, (2) much of what comes to the surface on a daily basis are habitual/automatic thoughts that reinforce your subconscious beliefs, and (3) the rest gets drowned out by the fast pace of living. However, when you learn to slow down just enough to start paying attention to your thoughts, you become increasingly self-aware. And with every thought you're aware of, you get to decide if it's a thought you'd like to think again. Remember, the thoughts you think over and over again become your belief system.

This chapter will help you shed light on habituated thought patterns and old belief systems that create and perpetuate burnout. With this new awareness, you can make the conscious choice to think and respond to yourself and the outer world in a new way.

As a rule of thumb, beware of unhelpful thoughts that make you feel as if you're defeated, constricted, or stuck in a rut. Helpful thoughts, on the other hand, feel expansive and nurture you through kindness; they reinforce self-trust in your growth potential. Through this process of changing your mind to create thought patterns that lift you out of burnout and facilitate long-term wellness, you will ask yourself, *Is this a helpful thought?* At first, the answer may not seem obvious. For example, your "inner critic" is a trickster than can have you believing you need to be tough on yourself to succeed. Yet, negative self-talk litters your mind with self-defeating messages, keeping you stuck, distracted, and disempowered.

Self-criticism doesn't serve you in any sustainable, helpful way. It can seem as though you need to be tough on yourself to motivate yourself to do better—but this only leads to burnout. As you learn to disengage with your self-criticisms, you can choose positive self-talk, and a new way of motivating yourself will emerge. You get to stand in your own power with self-confidence, feel great about yourself, and do great work.

Your mind has the capacity to make you out to be your friend, worst enemy, or something in between, like an estranged acquaintance you rarely see. Regardless, I know you're ready to "get out of your own way," so let's get reacquainted with who you really are—and that's your true best friend. The remainder of this chapter is dedicated to questioning old beliefs, choosing new ones, and learning practical strategies to create a whole new way of thinking. As you change your mind by believing helpful thoughts, you create the life that you want.

Our Internal Belief Systems

True freedom is untethered from all self-limiting beliefs. Societal definitions of success can, and do, limit people's beliefs and therefore potential. When we buy into someone else's definition of a worthy person, we rob ourselves of self-worth and the ability to be our personal best. Even the definition of personal best is tied to external markers and culturally derived limiting beliefs. In some very real ways, you may already be living your personal best, yet if it doesn't live up to someone else's expectations, it won't feel good enough. Since we live in a burnout culture, as long as we abide by the belief system of the masses, we will be at risk of burnout.

In our burnout culture, "scarcity" is the societal belief that there isn't enough good fortune, wealth, or success to go around. It's reinforced nearly everywhere you look: in the news, advertisements, the economic forecast, the political landscape, corporate culture, your place of work, and most likely your bank account. But it's not just about scarcity of money—it's the underlying sense that there's never enough: time, energy, resources, or information. We live in the age of information overload, yet the ability to absorb what's nurturing, real, and healthy for us often gets blocked by feelings of overwhelm and inadequacy.

We compensate for scarcity by grabbing, reaching, pushing, pulling, and forcing our way through life. Given the sense of urgency and competition to be the one person vying for the top position, life can feel like a game of catch-up. From that vantage point, you'll always feel like you're behind—constantly hustling, trying to prove yourself, being better, doing better—which creates an undercurrent of anxiety and panic. Unless you choose to think and then do things differently, your life will remain an exhausting and seemingly futile endeavor. The unhelpful thought, *I am not enough*, and its variations are at the root of the fear and disturbances that strongly contribute to burnout. The positive news is that with awareness you can change your thoughts. Exercise 15 is a great way to work with your thoughts and undo scarcity beliefs.

I DON'T HAVE ENOUGH...

Objective:

This exercise will help increase your awareness of how thoughts of scarcity and beliefs show up for you while building a willingness to think about yourself in a new way.

Time + Frequency:

Five minutes; one time daily for two weeks (ongoing daily as needed).

Directions:

STEP 1: Sit quietly and take a few breaths to ground yourself. Then, fill in the blank to finish this sentence: "I don't have enough . . .

_____

_____

_____ ."

STEP 2: Repeat the statement and notice how this thought feels in your body.

STEP 3: Next, follow a new train of thought: *What if I'm enough right now? What if I know I'm doing the best I can with the tools and information I have?* I know you aspire to learn and be more—but what if what you already know and are is enough in this moment? These questions are meant to be an open-ended self-inquiry, helping you notice how this new potential feels in your body.

STEP 4: Sit quietly for a few more breaths to complete the exercise.

Anytime you think, feel, or act from your "I don't have enough" sentence, you're in the scarcity mind-set, which leaves you feeling stuck and trapped by limited possibilities. This is a scary place to live—but what if you are enough, just as you are right now? The skewed standards of what is enough increases the pressure to live up to some invisible standard. What is the "enough" measure on a social scale? Who is enough? It's a preposterous and broken question, and it's not surprising that "imposter syndrome" is so common and goes hand-in-hand with burnout.

Burnout is the belief of scarcity in lived form, but you're more than that and you deserve better. You are *not* your burnout—it's simply the result of living in our culture and buying into its belief system. No one else has the power to control your beliefs, yet you've been persuaded to believe many things. And now, as you reevaluate through this process of recovery, you get to choose differently. The power to change your outcome begins in this present moment: you get to choose a new belief system and new thoughts that support "I am enough."

From the abundance vantage point, you are enough! You expand your growth potential when you can lovingly accept and start to believe that you're exactly who and where you are meant to be right now—and you'll be enough in a year, a decade, forty years, and so on. Even when you think about the past or plan for the future, your power is in knowing you're enough NOW. So, the question is: How do you want to think—right now—to function as the person you're becoming? Will you choose thoughts of scarcity ("I'm not enough") or abundance ("I'm enough right now")?

An abundance belief system supports helpful thoughts because anything is possible from a foundation of "I'm enough." All thoughts and beliefs that go against your well-being are simply no longer aligned with who you're becoming, and you get to choose different thoughts. Expansive beliefs full of potential can be created by simply thinking them over and over until new neural pathways have been formed. In this way, you are designing your life from the inside out. You get to make it as big and amazing as you want simply because you can, and you are SO worth it. To further understand the difference between unhelpful and helpful thoughts that either deplete or support your healthy growth, look at the chart on the following page as a guideline.

Imposter Syndrome

Imposter syndrome is a cluster of persistent feelings of inadequacy despite external markers of success. It has been documented that approximately 70 percent of people will experience at least one episode of imposter syndrome, and it's most prevalent among high achievers. The fear of being "found out" for not being as knowledgeable or capable as others expect you to be often results in pushing harder to make sure no one finds out you're a "fraud." But here's the thing: when you live with a sense of fear and lack (scarcity), there's no marker of external success that will ever be enough.

Unhelpful Thoughts	Helpful Thoughts
• Deflate mood and sense of worth	• Uplift mood and sense of worth
• Trick you into believing that punitive words are the best motivators	• Motivate you through kindness and positive self-talk
• Fuel the scarcity mind-set and mind traps	• Fuel the abundance mind-set
• Rev up the body and mind (turn on the sympathetic mode)	• Settle and quiet the body and mind (turn on the parasympathetic mode)
• Create disorganized and chaotic thoughts and feelings	• Create focus and clarity
• Are constrictive and keep you burnt out	• Are expansive and heal burnout

Mind Traps

The brain loves a good story with a clear beginning, middle, and end. It doesn't even have to be a "good" story, in which you come out on top. It just needs to have structure and a rational way to get from point A (the beginning) to point B (the outcome). The rational mind, driven to understand its surroundings, becomes scattered and disorganized when it doesn't have control over a situation. The unknown creates added stress in your mind and body as your brain attempts to make sense of the fast-paced, often unpredictable world, which prompts stress and drives burnout. Teaching your brain to let go of control releases burnout.

Keeping yourself busy and on task allows your mind to feel some sense of control; it understands the story line. You can do external tasks like a work project or you can make a mental tally of all your internal thoughts about the past and what you think may happen in the future. When an external task is completed, or a story about the past or future has run its course, your brain can momentarily settle as it thinks, *I am complete, safe, and know what is going on.*

This relief doesn't last long because your mind is always on the go. Reflected in your outer life, your mind is continually searching for answers and experiences with the desire to feel satiated, complete, and whole. By first becoming aware of the stories you create, you learn to understand how your brain is functioning. From there, you can reel in the story by returning your focus to the present moment. This retraining of how you use your brain will lead you out of "unhelpful stories" to stabilize your thoughts, regardless of where you are on your life journey.

Being in the throes of burnout is a confusing and painful time, and as you now know, your brain doesn't like to not know what's going on or to think about being in pain, so it tries to figure its way out of the intense discomfort. If there's no "story" to latch on to as your mind scans for answers, it simply makes one up. In an attempt to secure more control over any given situation, each story line takes on a habitual structure and rationale.

"Mind traps" are patterned ways of devising these made-up stories, which can become your "go-to story" in times of great distress. Mind traps trick you into believing they're helpful because there's a sense of safety in what you already know. But taking comfort in the discomfort of what you already know does you a disservice because it keeps you stuck in old thought forms. Remember to be kind to yourself as you begin to identify these mind traps within yourself. They've served a purpose in the past, but now you're shedding the old ways and it's time to choose differently.

Types of Mind Traps

Mind traps are known as *cognitive distortions* in Cognitive Behavioral Therapy (CBT). Mind traps keep you thinking in the same ways, coming to the same conclusions, and reliving the same problems. This happens because your brain likes consistency, and a mind trap—although ultimately limiting—is a predictable place to live. It's what your brain knows and feels comfortable with.

By reviewing the following mind traps, you'll start to liberate yourself from old patterned ways of thinking. As you read them, ask yourself which ones apply to you. In your daily life, begin to pay attention to how these mind traps play out in your interactions with yourself and with other people. Once again, be kind to yourself in this process; you've likely fallen into the trap of more than one of these common cognitive confines because it's a human thing to do. Yet now, as you familiarize yourself with these mind traps, you can change how you think and move away from these limiting belief patterns.

Mind Reader: Believing you know what someone else is thinking without checking in with them. You create a story about a comment that someone made or a look they gave you. But the truth is, your version of what someone was thinking or feeling in that moment is made up. The only thing you know for sure is what *you* think and how *you* feel about the situation in the present moment. Being a mindful observer of your thoughts, rather than an active participant who engages with them to build a larger story line, helps you recognize what feelings come up, and you can then choose to disengage from making up an elaborate story line. You can ask the person in question to clarify their reaction or response so that the superfluous act of mind reading is no longer necessary.

Catastrophizing: This is when you expect the worst to happen or you believe when something bad *does* happen it's the worst thing ever. When you catastrophize, your mind creates a story line that goes from bad to worse in increasing succession. As you go down this avenue of gloom and doom, your mind strengthens its belief that life has set you up to fail—so there's no point in trying to change. But you can work to stop this destructive spiral once you recognize that catastrophizing is just a thought pattern you're currently stuck in. "What if" statements are very common ways to catastrophize. An example is "What if I lose my job and I get evicted because I cannot pay rent?" Exercise 16 is an active way to help reorganize the brain to move toward thinking about better case scenarios.

SPIRALING UP!

Objective:

Sometimes it can feel all too easy to get caught in the downward spiral of distressing thoughts (catastrophizing), which leads you into further despair and becoming stuck in stress mode. But, what if there's another way? What if you can teach your mind and body to "spiral up" with a succession of helpful thoughts that lead to joy and endless possibility? This teaches you how to do just that.

Time + Frequency:

Ten minutes; three times per week for two weeks (ongoing as needed). Highly recommended to use steps 1 and 2 as a nightly journal prompt.

Directions:

STEP 1: Create a "what if" statement for something you worry about often.

What if _____

_____

_____

(*Example*: What if I bomb my presentation at work and get fired?)

STEP 2: Recreate the "what if" statement from step 1 into a better case scenario.

What if _____

_____

_____

(*Example*: What if I ace the presentation at work and get a promotion?)

STEP 3: Stand up, feel solid and grounded with your feet about hip-width apart and planted firmly on the ground. Feel the entire length of your body extend from the floor all the way up through the top of your head. Now, say the "what if" statement from step 1 (out loud or to yourself). Notice how this thought feels in your body. Then, switch to the "what if" statement from step 2 and notice how this changes your body's response.

STEP 4: Continue to repeat this second "what if" statement again and again, adding even better case scenarios as you reach for the best-case scenario you could imagine.

STEP 5: As you spiral up, get your body into the mix by jumping up and down or waving your arms in the air. Really get into it as you celebrate your life without limitations. Continue spiraling up for one to four minutes.

STEP 6: When you're done, stand quietly, close your eyes, and notice the changes in your mind, mood, and body.

Labeling: This is a way of name-calling that either discounts yourself or another person. You may find yourself saying, "I'm such an idiot" or "He's a total loser." Statements like this may feel justifiable in the moment, but they're very limiting and defeating ways to think of yourself or other people. The pull to label is strong, so I suggest you refer back to the unhelpful versus helpful thoughts chart (see page 74) to review the ways that name-calling can negatively impact your well-being.

Perfectionism: The believed lie that there's such a thing as one perfect way leads to perfectionism. Perfectionists believe that in order for something to be done well, it must be done right the first time without any mistakes. This story line stunts creativity, the willingness to take risks, try new things, speak your honest truth, or be kind to yourself. If you suffer from burnout, you are most likely a perfectionist. By practicing the change process outlined in this book you are learning how to release the need to do it "perfectly" the first time. I recommend that you keep this in mind as you learn how to cultivate practice over perfection.

Discounting and Filtering: This happens when you pay attention to negative events and/or discount positive experiences, by thinking that they're untrue or don't count. This strengthens a negative bias and creates the story line that nothing positive ever happens to you, and if by some chance it does, it only happened by fluke or luck. Self-defeating beliefs play a big role in this mind trap by convincing you that nothing good can happen to you because you don't deserve it. Is this a helpful way of thinking? Again, refer back to the chart on page 74 and decide for yourself.

All or Nothing: These thoughts frequently include absolutes and extreme rules or categories. Common words such as *always, never, completely, totally,* and *perfectly* are expressed in this thinking. It creates a very black-and-white story line, making something either "all good" or "all bad." This thought pattern creates an increasingly limited worldview of what's indeed possible. This mind trap, in particular, can be so automatic that you may not even notice it at first. As you begin to build awareness of your thoughts, I suggest listening for these assertions of absolutes.

Emotional Reasoning: This happens when you base your judgments, decisions, and conclusions exclusively on your feelings (especially when you're stressed) and believe that if you feel a certain way than it *must* be true. Once you calm down and reevaluate the situation, your viewpoint likely shifts. So, here it's about choosing to calm down prior to reacting to a situation, (i.e., don't send that email right away).

Regardless of which mind trap(s) you are stuck in, Exercise 17 provides a structured practice to rethink those habits for lasting change.

REWIRE YOUR BRAIN

Objective:

As you build awareness of your habitual thoughts, you can make the conscious choice to eliminate unhelpful thoughts by replacing them with helpful ones. When practiced consistently, this exercise will rewire your brain with helpful thought patterns that support your well-being.

Time + Frequency:

One minute; multiple times per day for two weeks (ongoing as it becomes a habit).

Directions:

STEP 1: When you become aware that you're engaged in a mind trap or are thinking an unhelpful thought, STOP right there and do the following:

STEP 2: Label the statement for what it is: *That's an unhelpful thought*, or *That's a false belief*, or *That's an old story that isn't helpful anymore*, or *That's a mind trap*.

STEP 3: Do a simple (general) reframe: *From now on, I choose only helpful thoughts that support my well-being.*

STEP 4: An optional, additional step is to then state a helpful thought that's specific to your situation.

Full Example:

You arrive to the train station just as your train is pulling away. You say with annoyance, *Ugh, I always miss the train!* You notice this thought, so you stop, and say, *That's an unhelpful thought.* And then you say, *From now on, I will only choose helpful thoughts that support my well-being.* You can even add, *Sometimes I catch the train on time. Actually, I did yesterday!*

"Should" Statements

The most common mind traps are "should statements." These are socially pervasive and unhelpful, and they only serve to perpetuate burnout. The word "should" creates an unkind and limiting thought, as it reinforces a strict set of rules for yourself and others. It works against self-acceptance and hinders your ability to choose another way. Each time you think or say, "I should . . .," you're essentially scolding yourself for not doing something in a certain prescribed way. Similarly, when someone else says, "You should . . .," it reinforces the internal self-judgment of "I'm doing life wrong." A whole slew of stories and feelings can arise over not living your life in the right way, always getting things wrong, second-guessing yourself, and mistrusting your own internal knowing.

Becoming aware of your use of the word "should" and its social pervasiveness can be an ideal teacher. There's no one right way to do life. And when you can remove "should" from your patterned way of thinking and speaking, you give yourself a huge gift. You practice self-kindness and open yourself up to accepting yourself as you are. From this point of acceptance, you can decide how you want to live, creating more helpful thoughts that support your recovery from burnout.

Laden in regret, wrongdoing, and judgment, "should" is one of the most overused and destructive words in the human language. Like any patterned way of thinking and talking, the word "should" is such a habitual way of communicating that it often goes unnoticed. However, you can make it a point to remove it from your own vernacular. The practice of removing this one word from your day-to-day has the power to profoundly shift how you think, feel, and act—opening you up to possibility and freeing you from old ways that keep you stuck and burnt out. Exercise 18 will help you release the burden of "should" in a practical and manageable format.

PHASING "SHOULD" OUT OF YOUR LIFE

Objective:

This three-part exercise teaches you to become aware of the social pervasiveness of the use of "should." You'll practice effective reframes that will become automatic thoughts in place of unhelpful "should" thoughts.

Time + Frequency:

One to five minutes daily for as long as it takes to phase "should" out of your life.

Directions:
Part 1:

Start to notice the pervasive use of "should" statements that you and other people make throughout your day. Also notice the emotions you link to these statements when you hear them (i.e., guilt, shame, regret). If you find it helpful, begin to keep a tally, marking off each time you say the word. Start a second tally for how often you hear it being used by someone else. Do this without judgment or condemnation, while remaining curious as you take stock of this social norm and how it affects your mood (do this for at least two days, in preparation for Part 2).

Part 2:

Begin to reframe your "should" statements. This can be done in two main ways:
(1) Replace "should" with "could," or
(2) Replace "should" with something like *It would likely benefit me if I . . .*
An example of optional reframes for *I should go to the gym* include:
(1) *I could go to the gym,* or
(2) *It would likely benefit me if I go to the gym.*

Part 3:

As you remain consistent with this reframe practice, you'll begin to notice when you're about to say "should" right before it happens. At this point, change it to "could" or another affirming phrase. You're now at the phase of consciously removing "should" from your habitual way of thinking and speaking—and you may be surprised at how easy this process becomes once you've become so aware. Record some of the "should" statements you noticed along with the reframes you used below.

(1) Should statement:

(2) Could reframe:

(3) Other reframe:

(1) Should statement:

(2) Could reframe:

(3) Other reframe:

(1) Should statement:

(2) Could reframe:

(3) Other reframe:

(1) Should statement:

(2) Could reframe:

(3) Other reframe:

Affirmations, Mantras, and Reframes

Everything we think or speak is an affirmation. We are affirming the thought as truth, whether we mean to or not, whether it's helpful or not. What do you actually want to affirm as your truth? Choose it. A mantra is another way to say an affirmation. I personally prefer to use the term "mantra" over affirmation, yet they are basically the same. Choosing to make a statement that aligns with your chosen truth and repeating the mantra/affirmation often reinforces helpful thoughts and beliefs. Further, reframes are a specific way to use chosen mantras/affirmations that are inserted right after you realize you made an unhelpful thought or statement and want to revise it.

The Three-Step Reframe:

1. Acknowledge to yourself (with kindness) that you made an unhelpful thought or statement.

2. Take a moment to pause with a breath.

3. Choose a new statement that affirms what you actually want to reinforce as a belief.

Here's an example:

Unhelpful affirmation: *I'm such an idiot!*
Helpful reframe: *Actually, I'm highly intelligent.*

This is an effective and active way to teach your brain to phase out unhelpful thoughts and build a habit of engaging with helpful thoughts and beliefs.

Learning + Choice

Humans exist in a perpetual state of learning, whether we're conscious of it or not. By simply being alive, we receive information through all of our senses and interpret it for ourselves. Through observation of our internal and external landscapes, the new information either reinforces prior learning to strengthen our beliefs, or we learn new ways of being. Neither is inherently right or wrong. The important thing is that we become conscious of what we think so we can choose what we want to strengthen and what we want to release.

Relearning doesn't require that you get rid of all your old ways of doing things. In fact, much of what you know is beneficial and will continue to be so. But there are unhelpful ways that keep you stuck as a smaller version of yourself that lead to burnout. This transformation isn't a forced process, but rather an exploration to be taken with courage and curiosity as you shed old layers that no longer serve you and reveal the new ones.

The power of growth and healing lies in the willingness to change your mind and believe that it's possible. Thoughts like "I can't" and accompanying self-doubt can surely creep up and make you feel like change is impossible. Yet, the science of neuroplasticity proves, without a doubt, that change can occur at any time in your life. Neuroplasticity is the brain's ability to reorganize itself by creating new neural pathways, while eliminating ones that are no longer necessary. The pathways that are used get bigger and become the superhighway for your thought patterns. The ones that are no longer reinforced begin to shrink, are deemed unnecessary, and eventually become obsolete.

TIP

Challenging old thoughts will bring up a lot of self-judgment, which is normal. Approach this process with kindness to yourself, knowing that what you're doing is revolutionary because you're going against the grain of social and familial norms and strongly held beliefs.

The "use-it-or-lose-it" idea is alive and well in neuroplasticity. This means that every time you choose a helpful, expansive, healing thought you strengthen those connections. Through the process of learning new concepts and practicing them repeatedly over time, these new ideas are reinforced and become your new way of thinking that supports a sustainable, burnout-free lifestyle. Learning any new skill takes focus, practice, and consistency. Over time it will become a habit—and your new normal.

In the early stages, this new way of thinking won't be easy, and that's okay and to be expected. This isn't a perfect process—and remember, thinking you *have* to be perfect will keep you from learning new things. You may find relief in this concept (a kind of "get out of jail free" card) or a bit terrifying (the out-of-control feeling of not doing something "perfectly"). Either way, it's normal to experience some resistance to change. And when you notice thoughts that tell you to

quit, recognize these as protectors that are trying to keep you safe. However, you're done with these old ways and can choose different thoughts that keep you growing into the person you truly want to be.

"I get to choose what I think" is a super empowering mantra. You're the expert on *you*. Deepening your belief in your own ability to fully know what is helpful and what is masked as helpful (self-criticism, scarcity beliefs, and mind traps) enables you to choose how you want to think and live. By working with these concepts and practicing the tools, you bring your own healing system—more and more—into focus. The heavy lifting comes at the beginning of transformation, since this is a process of relearning during which time you must be willing to suspend the need to know the exact outcome. Yes, your brain will scramble and get temporarily stuck in mind traps, but keep doing the work because you get to create your new story line.

Enhanced Focus + Mindfulness

What if you feel totally stuck and hopeless to make these vital mind changes? Your life is fast-paced, and your mind moves just as fast (maybe even faster), which can make you feel unfocused, disorganized, and chaotic. Life seems to be coming *at* you, and your thoughts are too many and too out of control to know how and where to begin. I'm here to tell you that with a little bit of practice, you can regain your power and effectively pay attention to your thoughts. As this happens, you will no longer be a passive recipient of habitual thoughts and socially patterned conditioning. You will become a "conscious consumer" of your thoughts, only buying into the ones you want to keep.

Sleep

Slowing down at the end of the day can bring on racing thoughts and physical symptoms of anxiety and panic (i.e., racing heart, constricted throat, belabored breath), which can make for a restless night's sleep. You can gain better sleep quality when you learn to quiet your mind chatter and rid yourself of the anxious feelings that manifest themselves in your body. I suggest creating a bedtime ritual that begins at least one hour before your planned bedtime. Start with putting your phone on airplane mode and then physically slowing your movements, perhaps choosing to take a warm bath with essential oils or sitting down to read your favorite book. This signals your mind and body that it's time to rest. If your mind is super busy, you can journal some "what if" statements (see steps 1 and 2 in Exercise 16 on page 77) to stamp out persistent and worry thoughts. Lastly, once you're lying in bed, I recommend you practice body-focused breathing (see Exercise 12 on page 58) to further soothe your body and mind through this deep awareness practice.

As you may recall from the last chapter, your mind is an accomplished time traveler, spending most of its time in the future or the past—looping and spinning in its own space-time continuum. It keeps itself busy ruminating on the past, worrying about the future, and making up stories that will never happen, all the while keeping thoughts far away from the present moment where these projections would disappear.

We tend to avoid the present moment because it feels so out of control—and your brain hates to lose control. But the irony is, when you regain focus in the present moment, you actually gain control over your thoughts and your brain can function at its optimal level. You may not know what's going to occur in the next moment, next week, or next year, but you can know what's happening

now—and there's safety and a sense of security in this awareness. When you train your brain to live in the here and now, you become completely aware of this moment, you know the outcome of now, and that's all your brain needs to feel organized and calm. Once the chaos has settled, there's no need to "time travel" away from the present moment. Focus is regained; you're no longer regretting past events or anticipating your life into the future. You can be with yourself now.

Since your body and breath are always in the present moment, when you place your focus there, your mind rejoins the present moment awareness. Every time you return to your body, you disrupt the habit of thought. And each time you disrupt this habit, you make it easier to slow down and stop the pesky and unhelpful thoughts. In this way, you teach your mind to remain present, focused, and on task. To do so, you can practice any of the body-awareness techniques you've learned so far (see chapter 2's Skill Take-Aways on page 67 for practice options) or Exercise 19, which specifically enhances brain functioning through the use of slow, mindful movements that teach the mind to keep pace with the body. It's a great way to wind down from your busy day when you're experiencing mental fogginess are trapped in racing thoughts.

MINDFUL SLOW-MO

Objective:

This is one of my favorite ways to relish the present moment at a slowed pace. Through your focused attention on the slow muscle movement of your body, you can retrain your mind to quiet down and stop "overthinking."

Time + Frequency:

Five to ten minutes; a minimum of five times per week for two weeks (ongoing as needed).

Directions:

STEP 1: While standing with your eyes open, begin to move and stretch your body in any way that feels good. Let your body intuitively take the lead. There's nothing to think about—just move and feel into the sensations of your stretched muscles.

STEP 2: When you're ready, begin to slow the movement down, mindfully observing (both the physical movement and the sensations) of your body in motion as it moves at an increasingly slower and slower pace.

STEP 3: Move as slowly as you can for as long as you want. If your awareness drifts, simply return your focus to your body's movement.

STEP 4: Next, try moving only one section of your body (such as your forearm through to your hand). While moving this area slowly, observe with curiosity.

STEP 5: To finish, slow your body into stillness, close your eyes, and simply notice how your mind, mood, and body have responded to this exercise.

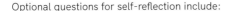

Optional questions for self-reflection include:

- How did this experience shift me internally?

- In what ways can I be more myself when I slow down?

- What are some other ways that I can inspire myself to become still?

- How can I bring what I'm learning here into my everyday life?

Chapter Summary

Your mind is a powerhouse of information that guides your beliefs and directly affects how you show up for yourself and within the world. As you increase moment-to-moment awareness of your thoughts, you begin to understand why you're feeling and behaving in certain ways, and get to choose how you want to proceed from this moment on.

In this chapter, you learned that unhelpful thoughts, including a scarcity mind-set, have become your automatic thought processes primarily because they are what society portrays as reality. Being susceptible to external messaging is normal, and it's how we learn about life, beginning with our parents, and outward into the larger social environment as we grow. Now, taking the same capacity to learn—backed by heightened awareness—you can master your own mind by creating new thoughts and beliefs.

It's that simple, and yet not so easy. It takes discipline and practice to focus your awareness on your thoughts and then to choose helpful thoughts that build new belief systems that support sustainable well-being and honor rest as much as action. You'll most likely slip into old patterns of thinking, especially during the first few months of this practice. Please know that each time you notice that you've gotten caught up in your old way of thinking is an opportunity to choose differently and strengthen your new way of thinking.

Thanks to the magic (and science) of neuroplasticity, our brains have the capacity to change at any time. And you're healing a little more each time you choose a helpful thought over an unhelpful one. Remember, all change occurs through the choices you make in the present moment. Especially when life feels extra busy and your thoughts get loud and disorganized, return to your ever-present body and breath to regain focus and change your mind for good.

Chapter Skill Take-Aways

Let's take a moment to review the different skills you have begun to practice, the reasons you want to keep practicing them, and how to keep using them most effectively for your healing and evolution.

- In a world that promotes scarcity that breeds Imposter Syndrome and feeds burnout, Exercise 15 *I Don't Have Enough . . .* is an important tool to gain clarity on how this messaging affects the way you think and feel about yourself. When you notice yourself say some version of *There is never enough . . .* , take this opportunity to choose a reframe that supports the belief and feeling that *I am enough right now.*

- Specific to the mind trap of catastrophizing, Exercise 16 *Spiraling Up!* builds your thoughts into ever-helpful, rather than ever-unhelpful, versions of your future. You can use Exercise 17 *Rewire Your Brain* any time you become aware that an old and unhelpful thought or mind trap has crept into your conscious mind. Exercise 18 *Phasing "Should" Out of Your Life* is a three-part practice that over a relatively short period of time will release you from the confines of rigid ideas of what is expected, allowing you to create life on your own terms with less stress.

- Working with movement, Exercise 19 *Mindful Slow-Mo* helps bypass the analytical thinking brain to quiet the busy mind and send a restorative message to the deeper levels of your subconscious. You may want to complete this thoughtful practice every night as part of your bedtime ritual for restful sleep.

Emotional Focus

Expressing your full range of emotions isn't socially acceptable. We learn early on that most emotions need to go underground, never to be seen again. This shutting down of our emotions begins at an early age, based on our family's belief system and social values around emotions. The bottom line is that no one has ever taught us how to fully feel our emotions. Yet when we can, life becomes so much bigger, more meaningful, and empowering.

Especially in the throes of burnout, your life can feel like an endless to-do list that's devoid of emotion or meaning. But being detached from your emotions isn't sustainable because emotions are meant to be acknowledged and felt—not locked away. The more you resist them, the more they persist. Burnout has a way of slowly revealing the emotions that you were never given permission to feel. The chronic stress of burnout comes full of hard emotions, including fear, anger, guilt, shame, numbness, and isolation. Continuously pushing these emotions away becomes increasingly exhausting. When you stop working so hard to keep them at bay and instead face your emotions, your exhaustion will begin to lift; you'll feel lighter and able to take on the world.

You'll also regain access to all of the delicious emotions that have been sitting dormant: you'll remember how to deeply feel love, joy, intimacy, elation, belonging, passion, and connectedness. Life will no longer be a list of tasks, but rather a truly lived experience. Let's take a moment to consider how society and your internal desire for preservation have shaped how you allow yourself to feel.

The most courageous and healing thing you can do for yourself is to start truly showing up for all of your emotions—you might even have to clear out the cobwebs (and skeletons) from the shadow spaces that you never go to. By using the tools in this book, and seeking professional support if needed, you will be able to process strong emotions—in essence, shining light into those dark areas. Like monsters under the bed, once you see them for what they are, they'll never seem as scary as what you feared. This means that you feel lighter, stronger, and more confident. When you have nothing to hide from yourself, you can no longer be an imposter. The rest of this chapter will teach you how to courageously work with your emotions in a healthy and sustainable way. In Exercise 20, reflect on and answer the questions using the list of emotions as a guide. I know that just the idea of *feeling* can be terrifying—but no need to worry. You've got this!

EMOTION IDENTIFICATION + ROOT RELATIONS

Objective:

This exercise is designed to help you identify your emotions and gain a deeper understanding of your current relationship with emotions.

Time + Frequency:

Fifteen minutes; one time. (Return as desired for further inquiry. Keep the emotions list handy and refer back often to build your daily emotional awareness practice.)

Directions:

Review the partial list of human emotions and write down your corresponding emotions to the following questions. If you don't see an emotion on the list, add your own. Keep this list as a visual guide and refer back to it as you learn to identify, allow, explore, feel, and release your emotions.

1. Which emotions were more allowed in your family?

2. Which emotions are most allowed in the workplace?

3. Which emotions do you allow yourself to openly feel in public?

5. Which emotions are lying just under the surface that you're trying not to feel?

4. Which emotions do you allow yourself to openly feel in private?

6. Which emotions do you want to feel, but lie dormant under burnout?

Accepted	Confused	Gratitude	Passionate
Affectionate	Contempt	Grief	Pleasure
Aggravated	Curious	Grouchy	Protected
Aggressive	Cynical	Guilty	Proud
Agitated	Delighted	Happy	Regret
Alarmed	Depressed	Hatred	Remorse
Amazed	Desire	Hesitant	Resentment
Ambivalent	Detached	Hopeful	Revulsion
Amused	Disappointed	Horrified	Sad
Angry	Disgust	Hostile	Scared
Annoyed	Doubtful	Humiliated	Shame
Anxious	Ecstatic	Hungry	Shy
Apathetic	Embarrassed	Insecure	Skeptical
Astonished	Empathy	Interested	Suffering
Attached	Enraged	Intimidated	Surprised
Attractive	Envious	Irritated	Suspicious
Belonging	Euphoric	Jealous	Sympathetic
Bitter	Excited	Joy	Tenderness
Blame	Exhilarated	Judgment	Terrified
Blissful	Expectant	Lonely	Unsafe
Bored	Fear	Love	Unsure
Buoyant	Fondness	Nervous	Vigilant
Caring	Forgiveness	Optimistic	Vulnerable
Cheerful	Frightened	Overwhelmed	Worried
Compassion	Furious	Panicky	Zealous
Confident	Gloomy	Paranoid	

Social Contracts

Even though humans are emotional beings, we've never been taught how to process our emotions—so a lot of funky stuff can happen when we relate to one another within a social context. Social contracts are unspoken, invisible, and interpersonal ways we interact with each other. They often deny us our feelings and keep us stuck. The strongest held social contracts are often between you and the people you most deeply care about, love, and/or strongly respect. Here's an example: you didn't let your sister know that her words upset you the other day. You didn't share your true feelings with her because she would feel bad, and you never want her to feel bad. So, you protect *her* feelings by trying to deny your own, all the while secretly harboring anger and resentment toward her.

Social contracts are limiting for everyone involved because they enable people to blame, judge, or use other tactics to deflect their emotions. You're responsible for your own feelings—and denying them or acting a certain way

so that other people won't feel bad perpetuates old patterns that no longer serve you. Emotional healing starts when you realize you've outgrown—or are willing to outgrow—your old way of handling emotions.

It's convenient to blame others for the pain you feel, but no one can make you feel a certain way, and blaming or verbally attacking others keeps you stuck. Other people's words and actions can trigger you, but it's your choice how to feel about them. Please know, all feelings are valid and important—it's simply about taking responsibility for your own emotions and allowing others to experience their own.

When it comes to burnout risk, social contracts are often related to the pressure to have it all together and the fear of "looking weak." Here is an all too common scenario: you never want to let your coworkers know how truly stressed you are or how overwhelmed and unsure you feel because you're afraid it will make you look like a poor performer and perhaps threaten your job security. Instead, you keep pushing harder to prove your competence—but this is at the detriment to your health and well-being. This dishonesty is harmful to both you and the people around you, because chances are they're pretending to be okay too, but in reality they're on the verge of burnout as well.

Social contracts serve a self-protective purpose. Yet, as you become aware that you're ignoring your emotions while enabling others to deny their own truths, you realize many of these contracts are no longer helpful. You can remove the armor—empowered to feel all the feels—and show up to your life as the fullest version of you.

Mismanaged and misunderstood emotions do everyone involved a disservice. The more you can own your emotions, the healthier you and your relationships will become. It's the process of becoming honest with yourself that gives you the confidence and power to be who *you* are. You're no longer at the mercy of someone else's ideas of who you are and how you "should" feel—and that's where your true power lies.

Helpful Truths about Emotions

Humans have an incredible capacity to feel—and it's when we can feel completely that we can live fully. The more we feel, the more we heal. Yet, feeling pain is both socially and instinctually uncomfortable. Since

> ### Self-Protection Is NOT Self-Healing
>
> Although your protective tactics served a purpose when you were a child, who had limited coping strategies, you've outgrown the need for this armor. As an adult, you're now safe to feel your emotions and self-heal.

we're hardwired to survive (recalling our reptilian brain and nervous system response to perceived threats), the (subconscious) message becomes clear: we must stay away from anything that brings any amount of pain. The good news is that we're consciously evolving beings who are moving beyond mere survival so we can thrive.

When you hold back your emotions or push them away, you're constricting and protecting yourself from being fully seen; however, this prevents deeper intimacy. Conversely, when you can fully process and express your emotions, you own your experience, which leads to empowerment and expansion.

An emotion is a felt sensation in your body that occurs when your brain releases a cascade of neurochemicals. Each emotion is made up of a unique chemical cocktail that enters your body. As you sense this physiological response, your brain is then able to identify and label it as a specific emotion. Think about this for a moment. When you feel happy, where do you feel it? Not in your mind—you feel it in your body.

Emotions + Responses

Emotions are normal responses to the lived human experience—and, they're temporary and can change quickly. The groundbreaking work of neuroanatomist Dr. Jill Bolte Taylor revealed that it takes a maximum of 90 seconds for the cascade of neurochemicals that make up any emotion to be flushed from your system. Like many of my clients recognize (and you probably do too), "I can handle pretty much anything for 90 seconds." Without knowledge of this, it's all too easy to believe that any uncomfortable emotion you have will last forever . . . and sometimes it really feels that way.

This is because when you're in the thick of it, difficult emotions usually last longer than a minute and a half.

And as you attach your thoughts to your emotional experience, your brain releases more neurochemicals into your body—each tacking on another 90 seconds until they're all flushed out. To take it one step further, when you link an emotion to a long-term memory or a story that you keep telling yourself, you ultimately train your mind and body to keep discharging the same neurochemicals—causing the disruptive sensation to linger for much longer. Being able to label your emotion is a good way to understand what's happening for you in the moment, but continuing to think about it and strongly identifying with a particular emotion for too long is unhelpful.

Emotions are *not* who you are; instead, they're experiences you have that are meant to be felt and then released. Your mind has a harder time letting go than your body does, even though it doesn't like pain. Therefore, over time your mind has learned different coping mechanisms to handle emotions. One such method is when your mind becomes completely enmeshed with an emotion, tricking you into thinking that you *are* the emotion. For example, you might say to yourself, *I'm anxious,* or *I'm sad*, and soon this is what your mind believes is the truth.

Another coping method is when your mind does anything it possibly can to avoid a strong emotion. Your mind will have you applying different distraction tactics to make sure you're not alone with your thoughts or emotions—anything to literally and metaphorically run away from the emotion. The tricky thing about this method is that it's only a Band-Aid treatment; denied or rejected emotions will always resurface. You can spend most of your time and energy pushing away strong emotions, without even realizing you're doing so. And the more you push away an emotion, the more exhausting it becomes.

When a strong emotion does return, you most likely revert back to the first mentioned coping method; you identify with it completely. As this feeling becomes unbearable, you then toggle between the two coping tactics (enmeshed and avoidant) while pretending everything is okay. On the outside it's "business as usual," while a war erupts inside of you.

But your emotions don't have to own you—there's fortunately another way. It's important to remind yourself that emotions are temporary and that they're *not* who you are, but rather an experience you're having. If you happen to feel sad or anxious, simply recognize it, instead of *becoming* it. This is the first step to feeling less sad or anxious. As you practice disengaging from the story lines of your emotions, you'll see that emotions come and go without major fanfare. They'll no longer run your life, and you get to choose how to respond to them, and even choose how to feel.

Emotional healing is about teaching yourself how to remain present with the physical sensation, without engaging the mind's coping strategies so you can retain your own power amidst any emotions. With practice, your body's ability to handle strong emotions will send a feedback loop to your brain that emotions are not made to hurt you—and therefore, you're safe to feel them.

Emotions help you heal and evolve by providing valuable information of your lived experiences that guide you in how you want to live. Although you cannot avoid emotions once you're experiencing them, you can learn how you want to live in a way that fosters more delightful feelings and less painful ones. When you're honest with yourself about your emotions, you learn what's working in your life and what you can change. In this way, emotions are part of your road map to becoming who you want to be. But first you must learn to identify and be with them. Exercise 21 provides steps to practicing this for 90-second intervals.

RELEASING EMOTIONS

Objective:

Since being overly identified with an emotion or avoiding it at all costs constricts your capacity to healthfully process your emotions, you'll now practice releasing your mind's need to take control for 90 seconds and learn how to let your body do what's needed to feel the emotion and then let it go.

Time + Frequency:

Two minutes; two times a day for two weeks (and as needed).

Directions:

STEP 1: Notice your current emotional state and set a timer for 90 seconds.

STEP 2: Label your current and predominant emotion (refer to the emotions list on page 93 for help).

STEP 3: Close your eyes and observe how the emotion is showing up as sensations in your body.

STEP 4: Breathe in and out of those sensations to create space between you and the emotion (remember the emotion is not *you*).

STEP 5: Each time you notice your mind wandering to a story about the emotion, return awareness to your breath and body.

STEP 6: Without force or expectation, allow the emotion to shift and move at will.

STEP 7: When the 90 seconds are up, spend a few moments to silently reflect.

Note:

You can practice this exercise any time you are triggered by a strong emotion or when you notice you are experiencing less intense or even enjoyable emotions. It's helpful to process mild emotions in preparation for managing highly distressing ones when they arise. The emotion will not necessarily "go away" within 90 seconds (although it very well might)! Remember, the purpose of this exercise is to practice being with your emotions for 90 seconds without the mind's coping strategies taking over to either overly identify with or deny them.

Change + Transformation

Change can feel lonely, confusing, alienating, and difficult to put into words; sharing what you are going through with others may also be hard, as well as relating to other people. Please know that this experience is common, normal, and a necessary part of transformation. You're outgrowing who you are, and you may even experience grief as you leave your old life behind. Simply being with these tough emotions and allowing them to exist without reflexively turning to one of your distraction or numbing strategies is a valuable lesson for self-growth. As stated earlier in this chapter, each of these emotional experiences will pass as long as you don't add any undue attention by attaching a story to them or pushing them away. The cyclical nature of change means that tough emotions like loneliness, confusion, alienation, doubt, and grief will come and go. And each time you complete a change cycle, your brain receives the message *I survived*, which provides the opportunity for your mind and body to create a new relationship with change. You'll increasingly become mentally flexible and expansive each time you make room for your emotions during times of change.

Habits + Choice for Healing

Just as you habitually move your body (including mannerisms and held tensions) and habitually think (including old beliefs and thought patterns), you also habitually feel your emotions. You become accustomed to certain emotions and hold on to them out of habit, which your body recognizes as a familiar blend of neurochemicals that are reinforced by the mental stories you connect to the emotions. Because of this process, you're actually reliant on your past emotional experiences. To end this cycle, you must stop allowing your past to dictate your life by making different choices in the present moment.

By learning to understand how you habitually feel and what your brain does with the information, you can begin to choose differently. Every habit you currently have was a choice you made at some point in time. Choosing to do the same thing over and over created this habit—but if it no longer aligns with who you want to be or how you want to live, then it's time to release it.

After awareness, the next step is making the *decision* to change. It's helpful that emotions rise and recede. You naturally want the good feelings to stick around forever and the ones that bring you pain to leave as quickly as possible. You also tend to forget the transitory nature of emotions when you're going through really hard times. During difficult times, it can seem like things have always been this way—or that you'll always be this way—and you stay stuck. But every moment in which an unwanted emotion arises is an opportunity to practice letting the emotion simply move through you. If you notice a story attached, watch with curiosity and label it as "story."

As you become aware of old, unhelpful messages, you can shift uncomfortable feelings to a more manageable level. In time, as habitual thoughts transform into helpful and supportive ones, so will your emotions. Burnout is a state of feeling stuck, and worry, anxiety, doubt, and unworthiness are some of the most common emotions that keep people stuck—and they are all rooted in fear. Let's unpack these emotions now and see where there may be some room for change.

Worry

Worrying won't fix a troubling situation—whether it's your or someone else's problem. Yet, there's a collective belief that worrying about someone shows that you care; this creates the illusion that you're doing something productive when life feels scary or uncertain. But while worrying may feel safe in its familiarity, it isn't helpful for anyone. When you can meet a person where they are with love, it's much more effective than worrying about them. You get to show you care without the added emotional baggage. Plus, worry is a huge time suck. Think about how much of your day you waste worrying or second-guessing yourself. In actuality, worry creates more worry, less action, lower productivity, and more self-judgment. It leaves you feeling stuck where you are—unable to grow, shift, or change. Since the habit of worrying grew over time and is tied to a social ideology and a bunch of self-defeating thoughts, it will take time and repetition to choose differently and create a new habit.

How to Change: When you catch yourself worrying for someone, remember how much you love and care about them. Focus on the love. When worrying in all other contexts, remind yourself that you're safe and ask, *How can I be kinder to myself right now?*

Anxiousness

Anxiety takes on a strong physiological response that can send your mind into panic mode. Varying symptoms of anxiety, like increased heart rate, rapid breathing (hyperventilation), sweaty palms, tightness in your chest, trembling, and feeling weak, tired, or unfocused, are followed by habitual thought patterns that add to the intensity of the experience. To make it even scarier, very "real" thoughts centered around ideas of mortality (*I think I'm dying* or *I'm having a heart attack*) flood your brain. The more often you experience anxiety, the more you fear it will happen again, which in turn increases the likelihood that it will.

How to Change: Once you can begin to understand that the physical response of anxiety is triggering the thoughts and further exacerbating it, you can begin to release its power over you. When you turn to your body as your salve, you can begin to heal from anxious feelings. Use Exercise 21 *Releasing Emotions* (see page 98) to help you ease feelings of anxiety.

Doubt + Unworthiness

Self-doubt hampers your creativity and your ability to show up fully as yourself each day. It also stunts growth and healing potential as it permeates and reinforces the belief that you're not worthy. Self-doubt keeps you stuck, as it gives you brain fog and is the ultimate dream killer, while self-assurance helps you build bigger dreams. Depending on how you look at it, simply being aware of the prevalence of imposter syndrome that we looked at earlier—in which many people at every professional level in every field experience the fear of being "found out" as a fraud that pushes them to try even harder to prove their worth (see the Imposter Syndrome box on page 73)—can reduce self-doubt's impact.

How to Change: Continue to trust in what you already know and worry less about what you don't know. And if there's something you want to learn—then go for it. But when you start from the foundation of "I am enough" (see Exercise 15 on page 72), then imposter syndrome is no longer an underlying and unhelpful driver in how you live and work. The most powerful thing that you can do is decide that you're enough.

Fear

The physiological response to burnout is a hijacked nervous system that thrusts you into survival mode, and this lack of safety translates into fear. Acknowledging your fear sheds light on it—allowing you to "see" it for what it is and heal. When you avoid, ignore, and deny fear, it's only temporarily misplaced, threatening to come back at any moment. And stuck stress is fear living in your body. It's that shortness of breath, holding your breath, or tightness in your throat that keeps you from sharing your opinions, and other habitual ways that you constrict and restrict yourself. These are some of the ways that fear shows up and limits your potential. Learning to know what fear feels like in your body is a necessary first step to healing; you'll be able to identify it when it arises and then utilize the awareness and release tools provided in this book. For example, my fear tends to live in my heart region as tightness and sometimes in my throat. Yet when fear has me in a lurch, it can show up as pain behind my eyes and stiffness behind my collar-bones. When I notice it, I also notice I'm either holding my breath or shallow breathing. Perhaps you can relate. Fear can "live" as stuck stress anywhere inside of you.

How to Change: When you notice fear, acknowledging it instantly removes some of its power. A helpful starter healing statement could be, *I'm feeling fear right now, and that's okay.* The truth is, you're going to spend some time in fear, since it's a strong emotion that lies deep within us as humans. Fear is the underlying root of all difficult emotions as it "hides" behind worry, anxiousness, and doubt, to name a few. When you get to the root emotion of fear, the prevalence of worry, anxiety, and doubt decreases. Therefore, when you can allow your fear to surface, you're able to heal on very deep levels. When you confront your fear, the "fear of fear" dissolves and you can then process life's stressors. Whether it's FOMO (Fear of Missing Out) or fear of not being good enough, facing your fears enables you to pass through them to the other side. In a real way, you must move through fear to get to peace. As you move along each step of the change process as you heal, grow, and evolve, your fears will resurface. And that's okay, because it shows you're moving in the right direction. The more you allow fear to be your teacher, the more liberated you'll feel. Let's now do Exercise 22, which will help you acknowledge fear within your body-mind system.

BODY + MIND AS ALLIES TO PROCESS FEAR

Objective:

Through this mantra-based exploratory practice, you will train your mind to work with your body in order to locate fear within you. You'll then consciously give it permission to be released.

Time + Frequency:

Five to ten minutes; four times per week for two weeks (ongoing to gain mastery, then brief version as needed).

Directions:

STEP 1: Say each of the following mantras to yourself and follow your own instructions. Between each mantra, pause and mindfully observe the response of your mind and body. Remain curious and observant.

1. *Through my mind, I allow fear to arise in my body.*

2. *Through my mind, I recognize the sensation in my body and label it as "fear."*

3. *Through my body, I breathe in and out of the fear spaces in my body.*

4. *Through my mind and body, I observe with curiosity how the breath creates space and shifts the presentation of fear in my body.*

5. *Through my mind, I reinforce the truth that in this very moment I am safe.*

6. *Through my mind, while remaining very grounded in my body, I allow the release of fear.*

STEP 2: Then say:

1. *Thank you, fear, for all the ways you have protected me.*

2. *I forgive you, fear, for all the ways you have helped me limit myself.*

3. *I no longer need you, fear, so I lovingly release you.*

4. *From now on, I acknowledge fear when it arises, and I'm open to love.*

Note:

As you become proficient at recognizing when you feel fear, you can use this brief version: *In this very moment, I am safe. Thank you, fear, for showing up to protect me. But, I don't need you anymore. Goodbye.* (You can even be silly and playful with the "goodbye," which further reduces fear's power.)

Connecting
Fear + "Should"

When fear is present, the ability to feel happiness, warmth, connection, love, and other life-affirming emotions is stunted. You may find yourself thinking, *I should be happier,* or *I should want to hang out with my best friend.* This will only make you feel worse than you did before, leading to the next logical thought, *What's wrong with me?*, as a cascade of new neurochemicals flood your body with a disparaging emotional state. There is nothing wrong with you: you're an impassioned, caring, connected person who has been temporarily cut off from your true essence by fear. This is one of the (many) areas where being kind to yourself is helpful. Instead of berating yourself with a narrative of all the reasons you're no good, you can acknowledge the truth: you're going through a challenging time that's triggering patterns that lead you into fear mode. From this point of view, you can choose a different thought, such as *I'm feeling fear right now, that's why I feel disconnected, and it will pass.*

Let's face the vulnerable truth head-on: most people don't feel good about themselves because they don't think kindly of themselves, and this creates a lot of fear-based behavior. Most people are trying to prove their worth in their professions, and because of this, they're doing things that bring on burnout: working extra hours, saying "yes" to everything and everyone, placing a crushing amount of pressure on themselves to do it all perfectly, and so much more. When you can adopt this truth with humaneness, then you can look around your work environment with great compassion for everyone, including yourself. This type of awareness requires courage to be deeply honest with yourself and to choose to think, feel, and behave differently. It's challenging work and totally worth it.

This is because the alternative is to live a fake "reality." When you're not living your truth, existence can feel plastic, uninspired, and disconnected. When I live in my truth, it feels real, free, possible. But when I fall back into fear-based belief patterns, I shut off, shut down, and block off things that seemed possible just yesterday. This is where keeping perspective is so vital—you need to remember the impermanence of all emotions and your ability to move, shift, and change at any time.

You're not fear—nor are you the fear you feel. You're simply experiencing fear. Yes, it's big, AND it's not you. Remember, you're not your emotions or thoughts—they make up an experience you're having. The more *aware* you become of these experiences, the more you will be able to be a conscious consumer of emotions and thoughts so that you can decide what you want to keep and what you want to release.

Just as phasing out unhelpful thoughts and reinforcing positive and kind self-talk strengthens mental capacity, choosing to reinforce nurturing emotions helps heal burnout. Emotions that foster healing include: self-kindness, self-compassion, self-forgiveness, gratitude, curiosity, nonattachment, and nonjudgment. Allow these self-healing emotions to be possible as you witness the emotions and connected thoughts that lead to more stress, anxiousness, worry, doubt, and fear. Being intentional about this process creates space to shift old beliefs and emotions toward the healing space of self-love, true joy, and true connection with yourself and the people in your life.

List of Healing Emotions

Similar to helpful thoughts, healing emotions enhance your well-being through a process of change that feels life-affirming. Here's a short list of some healing emotions:

Love	Joy	Gratitude
Appreciation	Curiosity	Wonder
Compassion	Kindness	Forgiveness
Playfulness	Acceptance	Worthiness
Wholeness	Limitless	Blessed
Nurtured	Loved	Prosperous

Judgment as a Litmus Test

Have you ever noticed that you're less judgmental when things are going well in your life? Some time ago, I realized this in myself, and I began to use my level of judgment as a self-awareness measure of the status of my well-being. When I found myself judging others, I knew that something disruptive was going on inside of me. Simply knowing this allowed for an openness to facilitate change and continue healing. Here's the thing: when you feel good, there's no subconscious need to judge others, since you're not judging yourself.

Self-acceptance, compassion, or cultivating any one of the healing emotions is a practice that lessens the desire to judge yourself and others. Each time you notice yourself judging someone else harshly, ask yourself, *What am I judging myself for right now?*

This allows for a new understanding and perspective of what's going on inside of you, strengthening your capacity for self-compassion as you decrease your judgment of others, and therefore judgment of yourself. In the process, you'll become more accepting of yourself, other people, and your surroundings.

Whether you notice yourself being judgmental or stuck in any old story that feels awful, learning how to become the objective observer will treat you well. It's another very user-friendly tool to work with your mind and body to choose another way. By practicing this new awareness in Exercise 23, you no longer need to rely on ineffective coping strategies. This tool will truly serve you far and well.

CAN I GET A WITNESS?

Objective:

This exercise teaches you how to gain perspective about your emotions by reinforcing the message within your body and mind that each emotion is part of your human experience, yet it's not who you are. Through this simple awareness meditation, you can be with any emotion without becoming either fully identified with it or trying to avoid it.

Time + Frequency:

Three to five minutes; one time daily for two weeks (recommended as an ongoing daily awareness practice).

Directions:

STEP 1: Begin seated with your eyes closed and notice your emotional state.

STEP 2: As you become aware of what you're feeling, say to yourself, *I'm aware that I'm feeling this way.**

STEP 3: After a few moments, add, *I'm aware that I'm aware that I'm feeling this way.*

STEP 4: Be with this new and expanded experience for a few more moments.

STEP 5: Begin to notice that from this vantage point you are an active yet neutral observer of your own experience, who recognizes the emotion is not you.

STEP 6: Be with this experience for as long as you'd like, and when you're ready, open your eyes and return to your day.

* *You can keep the feelings statement general as stated in the directions or substitute it with a specific emotion you're feeling, such as, "I'm aware that I'm feeling anger."*

Minding Your Emotions (Mind + Body + Breath)

Since your breath and body are your "present moment" teachers, they can alert you to when things aren't feeling right and serve as your safe base when your survival instinct kicks in and tries to have you escape your emotions. Especially in the beginning of this healing process, learning to consciously identify your emotions in stressful situations can be challenging. This is in part because the survival response occurs so quickly that a current emotion can go underground (into your unconscious) almost as fast. To gain consciousness of this suppressed emotion, you can turn to your breath and body.

The quality of your breathing is an indicator of how you're feeling. When you stop breathing (held breath) or breathe from your upper chest and throat (shallow breathing), it's a sign that you're experiencing some form of emotional distress; a stress-inducing saber-toothed tiger has sent your body and mind into self-protection mode. The situation feels too hard to bear, so you grip—physically and metaphorically—to hold on to yourself, as if this is what will keep you safe. This survival strategy has you forgetting to breathe as you hold on. However, this tactic only closes you off more, reinforcing the belief that you're under attack and must retreat.

An Act of Celebration!

Becoming aware of your emotions, how they affect your breathing, and the ways they show up in your body is a prime time to celebrate. Yes, you can absolutely celebrate in those moments when you're breathing well, your body feels relaxed, and your emotions are elevated. Also, it's just as valuable to celebrate awareness of the connection between your breath and emotions—when you're struggling—because it facilitates greater healing potential.

It seems to be that as we age, we tend to breathe shallower, keeping our breath held in one area. The subconscious belief is that if you can keep your breath contained, you can control what's happening. As the days and years go on, life can feel less and less manageable, so you will tend to close off more and constrict, which results in more held and shallower breaths. It masquerades as a sense of control, yet it has the opposite effect—the more you vie for control, the less control you have.

It may seem counterintuitive that the opposite of these constrictive actions is what will help you feel protected, safe, and in control. But science tells us that breath cycles with a longer exhale than inhale turn on your body's "relaxation response" (the parasympathetic mode). Research has also found that most people who experience anxiety have a reverse breathing cycle, with longer inhales and shorter exhales. Teaching yourself to breathe with a rhythm of shorter inhales and longer exhales mitigates stress and anxiety. From this more restful state, you'll no longer be in survival mode and your emotions will rise to the surface to be processed.

Whether you want to lower stress levels or process new emotions, this new way of breathing can be done anywhere, and at any time. With a bit of practice, you can learn to do this in any stressful situation, like the middle of an important client meeting

(when self-doubt rears its ugly head). Think of your breath as your secret superpower that allows you to feel calm, confident, and focused. You'll be able to stand in your power with the autonomy to show up as who you are and with all of your emotions, knowing you can handle anything that comes your way. Practice Exercise 24 often to make it your go-to breath rhythm.

TIP

Breath plus body awareness truly is the best medicine, but there may be times when your emotions are so big that you need to use a distraction or numbing technique. This may be scrolling incessantly through social media, having an extra glass of wine, or eating a bit too much . . . and this is okay to do sometimes. The important thing is to be conscious of your distraction/numbing choice: be aware of the reason for your current action (the underlying emotions), allow yourself to self-soothe in this manner, and do not beat yourself up for it afterward. Remind yourself that your emotions aren't always this intense, and next time you can choose differently.

PRACTICE BREATHING WELL

Objective:

By choosing to practice a breathing style with an extended exhale, you're consciously turning on your body's relaxation response and undoing the habit of shallow and held breath. The more you practice, the more in tune you will become to your breath. You'll get better at identifying when you're out of sync, and therefore experiencing distressing emotions, and you can return to breathing well. You may experience the calming effects after this very first practice. If not, that's completely okay and normal. Just remember to stay open, curious, and reflective with each practice.

Time + Frequency:

Three minutes; two times per day as a scheduled meditation and/or situationally for two weeks (ongoing as needed).

Directions:

STEP 1: Wherever you are, begin to notice your breath. Are you holding your breath, are you breathing in your upper chest and throat, or are you breathing deeper into your lungs? Without judgment, simply notice.

STEP 2: Consciously and slowly breathe *out* of your nose (you're starting the breath cycle with an exhale).

STEP 3: Breathe in and through your nose for a count of three.

STEP 4: Breathe out and through your nose for a count of five.*

STEP 5: Continue with this breathing pattern.

STEP 6: As you get acquainted with this breathing pattern, notice if you can extend your breath even further down into your lungs for a deeper breath.

STEP 7: To finish, release focus from your breath. Remain quiet and notice the aftereffects in your mind, emotions, and physical body.

The count can vary based on what works for you; just make sure the exhale count is a higher number than the inhale count.

You may find yourself in stressful situations where your "felt fear" (anxiousness, worry, doubt) doesn't pass as quickly as you'd like, despite performing focused breathing. At this point, the strategy is to accept how you're feeling, keep breathing well, and choose to take action. Acknowledging your stressed emotional state and consciously doing what scares you anyway reinforces within your body and mind that strong emotions don't have the power to debilitate you. The new pattern of neurobiological conditioning becomes: *My emotions don't control me, nor do they own me. They aren't who I am, and I can live a meaningful life with whatever emotions arise.*

Next-Level Healing

Once you've become aware of and stopped suppressing difficult emotions as you learn to move through them, you get to really choose the emotions you want to feel . . . but not before. If you were to deny or keep pushing the hard emotions away—putting on a fake smile and telling yourself and the world that you're "fine"—this would only escalate burnout. Real happiness and healing cannot happen when you're too busy behind the scenes hiding all of the socially unacceptable and uncomfortable feelings. To repeat: you must feel to heal! This is why you cannot bypass your emotions

and choose "only happy ones." This final section of the chapter is to be contextualized and practiced once you feel you have begun to embody the earlier emotional healing concepts.

The more you can accept who you are *now* and honor how you feel, the more you will deepen into your truest self, empowered to choose healing over self-preservation. This not only helps you recover from burnout, but it also makes you resistant to future risk of burnout relapse as you take charge of your life and continue to excel.

I believe that love, joy, and fulfillment are human birthrights and any limiting beliefs that create difficult emotions block us from who we really are. I also believe that we're born to learn, grow, and evolve by moving through these limitations. Referred to in the book's introduction as the human condition, our wounds and coping mechanisms have served a purpose.

And as you gain effective tools that deepen your understanding of your true worthiness and sense of safety, you can begin to shed the pain.

You can choose to avoid and resist, which would slow the process, or you can choose to be with what arises, without buying into old beliefs or old ways of feeling as you continue to heal and become more aware and elevated in your human potential. Everything you're doing now is not only healing your burnout but is also building the skills you need to keep upleveling your life through self-awareness that cultivates a deeper sense of Inner Knowing. Exercise 25 helps you stay centered in your emotional awareness while effectively and authentically shifting you into higher mood states.

Every moment offers the chance to live your life as the most honest expression of you. As your mind and body move out of the survival mode of burnout, you'll reveal more of who you are. And as you feel safer within your body, you'll trust that all of your emotions have benevolent intent—letting them rise to the surface and leave at their will. This awareness will help decrease your constant need to self-protect as you choose healing emotions. By basking in the light of this Inner Knowing, your body and mind reinforce that you're safe, whole, worthy, and available for life. Be still with this joy and balance, knowing it's from here that the courage to live life on *your* terms becomes your existence.

I urge you to use this book as a way to deepen your innate understanding of yourself. Your Inner Knowing will grow larger and brighter with practice over time. Although this innate knowing can make room for self-doubt and fear, it doesn't promote or enable it. Every time these types of feelings show up, realize that you've temporarily stepped out of alignment with the deepest parts of who you are. You can thank these feelings for showing up to protect you; forgive them for all of the ways they've limited your potential and kindly invite them to leave, as you return to your innate knowing that fosters elevated emotions and growth potential.

UPLEVEL YOUR MOOD TO UPLEVEL YOUR LIFE

Objective:

This practice enables acknowledgment, appreciation, and release of depleting emotions, while authentically transitioning to a preferred feeling.

Time + Frequency:

Five minutes; three times per week for one week. Make it a regular practice once you've gained a solid feel for the earlier emotion-processing exercises.

Directions:

STEP 1: Notice when a depleting emotion arises (i.e., fear, judgment, doubt, worry).

STEP 2: Notice whether it accompanies a certain thought or external situation.

STEP 3: Become aware that you're aware of this experience.

STEP 4: Get curious and allow it to exist as an awareness.

STEP 5: Choose gratitude for the depleting emotion, knowing it has served to protect you in the past and has risen to the surface of your consciousness to now be released. Truly be with this feeling of gratitude for a few moments.

STEP 6: Decide how you want to feel in this moment and choose that healing emotion.

STEP 7: Be with this elevated emotion for a few more moments and, when ready, continue with your day and notice with curiosity whether this new emotion lingers.

Quick Version:

Become aware that you're experiencing a depleting emotion. Get curious and allow it to be there. Transition to gratitude and then move on to your chosen emotion.

Chapter Summary

Emotions are a gift that allow us to feel truly alive and help guide us in choosing how we want to live and deepen our sense of Inner Knowing. However, having emotions means that we can feel deep pain, and our socialized and biological survival instinct is to avoid this discomfort. So, we protect by gripping, hiding, and becoming enveloped by our emotions, and this fosters burnout.

Burnout shows up in how you feel about yourself and carries over into how you interact socially within the work environment, your family, and other external arenas. By getting clearer on the ways that you stunt your ability to truly feel—while still feeling all the feels—you shift your relationship with yourself as well as within your external world.

You're now more capable of being with your emotions and processing them in real time. Once again returning to your breath and body as wise teachers, you can access more of your emotions and learn how to move through them with much less fanfare. As you learn to connect your mind, body, and breath in the present moment, they will serve as revealers and active healers, guiding you along the path of sustained well-being.

As you become more proficient at identifying your emotions—without getting stuck in or bypassing them—you can consciously process them rather quickly. With this new level of autonomy, no adverse emotion can stand in your way from deepening the knowledge of who you truly are and choosing to live an amazing life. This is because you can now move through any fear that naturally arises with change, aligning yourself with the healing presence of love, joy, and peace.

Chapter Skill Take-Aways

I feel excited for you as you experience this process of self-discovery. Will it always be easy? No, but it's worth it. The skills in this chapter teach you how to experience and manage your emotions efficiently and effectively while deepening self-authenticity:

- Exercise 20 *Emotion Identification + Root Relations* is a two-part inquiry into first labeling your emotion and then gaining a deeper understanding of your relationship to it on both a personal and a social level. Both parts can be returned to at any time, but I suggest that you keep the list of emotions handy so you can refer back to it often as you gain fuller awareness of your changing emotional states on a daily basis.

- Given that each emotion is the result of a cascade of neurochemicals that produces physiological sensations in your body—and that these chemicals are flushed out of your system within 90 seconds if you don't attach additional meaning through your thoughts to the experience—then Exercise 21 *Releasing Emotions* is a tremendously effective tool to retain focus on your body and breath as the sensations move through you.

- As you work with your powerful mind to enhance emotional processing within your body and breath, your whole system aligns to deepen consciousness of healing and of who you are. Exercise 22 *Body + Mind as Allies to Process Fear,* Exercise 23 *Can I Get a Witness?,* and Exercise 24 *Practice Breathing Well* work with this unity to help you stay present and then release your emotions in preparation for the advanced practice of Exercise 25 *Uplevel Your Mood to Uplevel Your Life.*

Chapter 5

Social + Personal Focus

Whether you realize it or not, there are underlying social values that support how you think, feel, and behave. Social values are a set of principles defined by traditions, institutions, and cultural beliefs that are often taken for granted as unquestioned societal norms. They serve a purpose and orientate us as individuals within a larger group. Social values are not necessarily a good or bad thing, but you need to decide whether they align with how you want to live. If you follow social values blindly, they can have negative consequences on your personal development and overall well-being.

In our ever-increasingly, fast-paced, and on-demand lives, the message is clear: produce more, show how much you're producing, make sure you look good doing it, and—by any means necessary—don't allow anyone to see your vulnerabilities, nor your exhaustion or actual human experience. Because society equates being vulnerable or weak with failure, the underlying message is that you better toughen up, work harder, and never ask for help. You're expected, at the minimum, to keep your current pace or to speed up.

Sadly, this burnout mentality continues to serve as a success marker, and although it may seem rational, it's insane and *not* sustainable. Humans are designed to be active, creative, innovative, and purposeful. We're also designed to rest, sleep, and enjoy valuable social time with family, friends, and community. Without balance, our social values are slowly killing us and furthering the distance between who we want to be and who we have to become. Burnout is, in essence, a disidentification from self, and the longer you're sucked into social values that support this "steamroll your way through life" mentality, the less chance you have of simply being you.

Life + Your Truth

Choosing to live your life aligned with your truth, not within the confines of social norms, is a challenging change process. It will push up against old beliefs and bring up self-protective thought patterns and uncomfortable emotions. This is why I provided you with practice tools in earlier chapters to get you started. You now have what you need to work with unhelpful thoughts and strong emotions so you can step into who you're becoming with greater confidence and ease.

Adulting + Burnout

I often hear from clients, as well as a general malaise among adult people, that "life is only going to get harder from here." This makes a lot of sense, given our current trajectory as a society of constantly pushing harder and harder; if you stay on the "gotta work harder to succeed" track, you'll continue to build a life that gets consistently harder. But when you pivot your perspective and are willing to create both internal and external changes, life won't be so hard. Choosing values that support a slower pace enhances mental clarity and energy so you can be more engaged with the life that you want to live. Let's look at some commonly perceived pitfalls of "adulting" that contribute to burnout and different ways to avoid them.

Adulting Myth 1: Busyness

Social values can be so ingrained that it seems preposterous to do it another way, even when it's obviously not working, which brings us to the paradox and addiction of busyness. Staying constantly busy creates the false perception that you're being productive and doing stuff that matters. This isn't to say that you're not being productive or what you do is meaningless. But when you buy into the social value of busyness, you actually become less effective at what you do, and the meaning tends to get lost. People often keep busy for busy's sake.

An aspect of burnout is the art of being busy. It keeps you stuck, feeling trapped in a perpetual cycle of anxiety and stress that seems impossible to sustain, yet never-ending. Can you relate? Like all addictions, there's a downside, and if you're willing to look into the shadows, you'll find a deeper truth. The truth is you don't *want* to be busy all the time. You don't *want* your head buzzing as you "do" and "go" at such a rapid rate. It feels out of control, doesn't it? On the other hand, if you weren't so busy, what would you be doing? Does the idea of slowing down and having moments in the day when you're doing "nothing" totally freak you out? If this is your experience, please know that it's normal and that you're not alone. Everyone who experiences burnout places a high value on busyness and has an underlying fear of slowing down. The slower pace makes room for all of the things you've been shoving away.

How to Change: Slowing down means dealing with your tough emotions and unruly thoughts, so it's no wonder why you stay busy. Yet, when you stop buying into the social value that busyness is a marker of being a productive or successful adult, you can show up for yourself fully in order to heal burnout. You must make room for all of your emotions and work with your thoughts and belief systems in order to face what's really happening and choose differently. And although this may sound like no fun, the rewards of being able to create a foundation of continued health and growth are truly worth it. In Exercise 26 you will observe your internal busyness while proactively shifting to a calmer state of engagement.

Adulting Myth 2: Seriousness

Do you believe that in order to be taken seriously you have to act serious? The social values of adulting identify "silliness" as no longer socially acceptable. To some, silliness is even equated with being unintelligent or naive. Yet, here's a question to ponder: can you be silly, sincere, sophisticated, and smart? My personal experience is a resounding YES! Humans are dynamic and complex beings. We're more than one thing, and definitely not only one thing at a time. Aspects of maturity include being able to maintain seemingly contradictory aspects of self as your truth; you can be serious and silly at the same time or at distinct moments.

How to Change: The point here is to resist the need to fit into a set of rigid standards that don't feel like you. Allow yourself to be flexible in who you think you are with a willingness to shift and change based on your internal guidance. When I teach workshops, I often lead participants through Exercise 27 that begins by releasing tension with slow, mindful stretching, and it invariably ends with laughter and lightness. The main takeaway is this: adults love to be silly, but social values tell them it's not okay, so they stop being playful and silly.

REWORKING BUSYNESS

Objective:

Busyness is a habit that keeps you going at a pace, and in a manner, that's not sustainable, reduces overall productivity, and is mentally exhausting. You can have a full schedule without the felt sense of being busy; it just takes some rewiring of your mind and body to shift your mind-set from "busyness equals effectiveness" to one that offers a calmer solution. This exercise helps create this new perspective, as you slow your nervous system down in the face of intensity.

Time + Frequency:

Five to ten minutes; one time per day for one week (ongoing as needed).

Directions:

STEP 1: Sit quietly with your eyes closed for one minute and watch your thoughts. Don't try to halt them in any way. Simply observe with nonjudgment as you notice all the types of thoughts that come and at what speed and intensity.

STEP 2: Stand up and begin to move your body in a way that matches the pace and intensity of your thoughts. Thrash your arms and body around (stomp your feet, hop around, bob your head) as much as you can with your eyes open so you don't bump into anything. Do this for a full minute, making your body as busy as you possible can.

STEP 3: Then stop! Close your eyes with your feet placed firmly on the ground, standing tall, with one hand on your heart and one hand on your belly. Be still and breathe until your heart rate returns to resting state.

STEP 4: Self-reflect on your experience from intense action (busyness) into stillness. Optional questions include: *What if all of the busyness stopped and the pause button hit in the midst of a workday frenzy? What would I see? What is actually going on? What could I get rid of? What do I want to keep?*

STEP 5: Take a full breath, and on the exhale "un-pause." Now go do the things you want to keep.

ENCOURAGING SILLINESS

Objective:

Gathering from informal surveys of my workshop participants, it's near unanimous that people love to be silly. Yet most adults stop allowing themselves to be silly. This exercise will remind you how fun it is to be silly and encourage you to be sillier more often, which in and of itself is a great stress reliever! After this exercise, you'll not only feel freer, but you'll also reinforce to your body and mind that your values don't necessarily align with the constraints of prescribed social values. You can be you and be an adult.

Time + Frequency:

Following one week of practicing Exercise 26 *Reworking Busyness*, focus on this exercise for eight minutes; one time daily for one week (ongoing as needed).

Directions:

STEP 1: Do Exercise 19 *Mindful Slow-Mo* on page 87 through step 4.

STEP 2: Then, instead of "slow your body into stillness" of step 5, move your body into silliness.

STEP 3: Move in as many bizarre and unexpected ways that you can come up with. Allow your mind and body to work in tandem as you move in sillier and sillier ways.

STEP 4: Allow yourself to laugh, make weird noises and funny faces, smile, and enjoy.

STEP 5: To finish, stand with your eyes closed and feel into the resonance of this experience.

Adulting Myth 3: Self-Reliance + Selflessness

One of the biggest rules to adulting that's a flat-out lie and keeps people feeling burnt out is that it's not acceptable to ask for help. It's this idea that once you reach a certain age, you no longer need help, and if you need to ask for it then you've somehow failed. Self-reliance in many ways can be an asset, and taking responsibility for yourself is truly a sign of health and maturity. But this is different than hiding the fact that things have become too overwhelming to handle on your own. The interesting dichotomy here is that although you're expected to take care of yourself, prioritizing self through self-care can be equated with selfishness. You're not supposed to ask for help, but you're supposed to be there for everyone else. Yet, being all things to all people is straight up exhausting—and you compromise who you are in the process. Over time, you'll forget who you are and what's important to you as everyone else's priorities become yours. And if this is the social norm and everyone's doing it, who's really helping whom, and to what end? Is everyone just helping each other live busier lives as we all lose sight of what really matters?

How to Change: Step out of your comfort zone and start prioritizing *you*. Allow yourself to say "No" to people and situations that drain your energy and overbook you. This way, you can say "Yes" to the rest! I'm talking boundary setting here, and it can be one of the hardest hurdles to overcome when healing from burnout. Further discussion and Exercise 31 are provided later in this chapter (see pages 133 to 135) to help you master this very important skill.

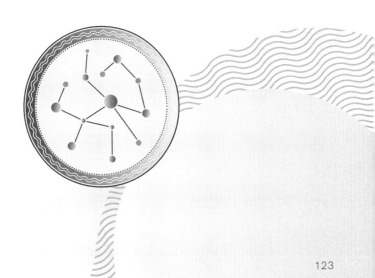

Adulting Myth 4: Universal Milestones

Adulting is often based on other people's ideas of how you're supposed to live your life, pontificated with a strict set of socially valued milestones. Most people don't reach these steps in a prescribed way because life isn't that linear. Yet the crushing pressure to "be further along in life than I am" is a heavy burden that many people carry. This creates a sense of always being behind the curve in a constant game of catch-up. Looking around, you compare yourself to others, further strengthening the belief that your life and what you're doing isn't enough. This isn't only a slippery slope, but also an incorrect measure of who you are. When comparing yourself to others, your barometer is based on outside standards of success that may not truly be your own.

How to Change: The definition of success is ultimately a personal one. When you're able to become clear on which social values you want to keep and which new values you want to embrace, you are defining more of what truly matters you. It's then that you can create a personalized road map to meet all of your chosen, personally valued milestones.

Personal Values

Your "why" is the underlying driver of everything you do. And in order to choose how you want to live, you must get clear on what this is. It could be an overarching "why," such as finding your life purpose, or an everyday "why," like deciding whether to go to the gym after work. Either way, as you gain clarity and prioritize what you want and need, you can more effectively build the life you want. The choice is yours on a moment-to-moment basis; present moment awareness helps you become clear on your current actions and provides a vantage point for "big picture" planning as you set your sights on your future.

You're ambitious and want to create a really amazing life, yet burnout has led you astray. This most likely occurred because you got caught up in the social values that keep people stuck and burnt out. Therefore, reclaiming or redefining your "why" by selecting

and prioritizing your own values is an important step in healing burnout and living a life of deep meaning for you. As humans, there are three ways we are guided and find reason for being:

- We adopt what's socially accepted and expected of us (social values system)
- We do it to avoid pain (human instinct)
- We align with our personal values (heartfelt principles and desires)

If we aren't paying attention, it's easy to get swept up in a life that happens because we go along with what's expected of us and to avoid pain. As discussed before, this survivalist tactic, although it keeps you from dying, isn't fully living. It's quite possible that some of your values align with social values. Yet, it's vital to get clear on your own personal values so you can start to question social norms that don't feel right to you. There may also be times when delaying a painful situation is appropriate. But since pain avoidance is not a long-term solution and it will keep you burnt out, you'll have to figure out another way.

Your personal values, beyond self-preservation, will guide you. This means showing up for yourself to live your fullest potential. It's easier to play small, do what's expected, and take fewer risks. It's time to change that.

Fear will surface, and so will your inner critic. But you must give yourself permission to not know everything. No one knows everything; there's simply too much information available for that to be true. No one is able to do everything perfectly the first time either. You're designed to learn, grow, and change. You'll fall down and get back up again—just like you did as a baby learning to walk. There's no shame in falling as you try, fail, and get back up again. Knowing where you want to go and why that is helps you build resiliency as you change your life. You can start by identifying and prioritizing your current personal values with Exercise 28.

TIP

Remember back at the very beginning of this book when we discussed the human condition? This applies here! As you courageously show up for yourself, rather than society, you recognize your humanness in real ways and allow it to be your asset rather than a shameful part that needs to stay hidden.

GETTING CLEAR ON YOUR "WHY"

Objective:

By working with this exercise, you'll be able to clarify and prioritize your heartfelt personal values that support your meaningful life.

Time + Frequency:

Fifteen minutes; one time (revisit as often as needed).

Directions:

STEP 1: Thoughtfully review the list of personal values on the opposite page.

STEP 2: Circle the values that are important to you right now (or add ones not already listed in the blank spaces).

STEP 3: Highlight or check off ten values that are very important to you.

STEP 4: Rank these ten from most to least important, with number one being the MOST important to you.

STEP 5: Having chosen your current values, do a little self-reflection on the exercise: *What came up for you? Were there any surprises? In what ways are you already aligned with your values?*

STEP 6: Next, consider how you can move forward from here: *What can you begin to let go of? What can you shift or change in your day that will align yourself more with your values?*

Acceptance	Expressive	Love	Sensitivity
Accountability	Fairness	Loyalty	Simplicity
Accuracy	Family	Mastery	Sincerity
Achievement	Famous	Maturity	Solitude
Adaptability	Focus	Meaning	Spirituality
Assertiveness	Freedom	Moderation	Spontaneous
Attentiveness	Friendship	Motivation	Stability
Balance	Fun	Openness	Teamwork
Beauty	Generosity	Optimism	Thoughtful
Boldness	Genuineness	Organization	Timeliness
Calm	Grace	Originality	Traditional
Capable	Gratitude	Passion	Transparency
Challenge	Growth	Patience	Trust
Charity	Harmony	Performance	Uniqueness
Clarity	Health	Persistence	Vitality
Clever	Honesty	Playfulness	Wealth
Comfort	Honor	Poise	Winning
Commitment	Imagination	Potential	Wisdom
Communication	Independence	Productivity	Wonder
Community	Individuality	Professionalism	
Compassion	Innovation	Prosperity	**Others:**
Connection	Insightful	Purpose	
Consistency	Integrity	Quality	
Creativity	Intelligence	Realistic	
Curiosity	Intimacy	Recognition	
Dedication	Joy	Recreation	
Dignity	Justice	Reflective	
Discipline	Kindness	Respect	
Drive	Knowledge	Responsibility	
Efficiency	Lawful	Risk	
Empathy	Leadership	Satisfaction	
Ethical	Logic	Security	

As you work with the previous exercise and continue to clarify and understand your personal values, keep the following ideas in mind. Personal values are the principles that really light you up inside. They will bring up life-affirming emotions, as Inner Knowing is accessed through your body. In this very real way, your personal values set the inner tone of your "why" and are guideposts to help you make conscious decisions for how you want to live. As you ask yourself what your current values are, be aware of when you're leaning toward ones that "sound good" or that you think you "should" have, yet don't really resonate. Refrain from choosing those. A clarifying question can be, *What really calls and tugs at me?* When you ask yourself this, you're less likely to choose personal values based on longstanding social values as you tune in to your inner sense of knowing.

TIP

Personal values are fluid and changeable. What you identify as a value today may not have been the same two weeks ago and may even change tomorrow. There's no pressure to get it right. The important thing is to check in with yourself and be as honest as possible to gain clarity and begin to prioritize what truly matters to you now.

Choose *You* + Own It

Be you or be like everybody else. By using your personal values as an anchor, you can more confidently choose *you*. Seeking outside approval and validation will only leave you feeling untethered and often undervalued, as it misrepresents the full scope of who you are. For example, if you're valued for being a good listener, or for closing the most deals, or being a member of an exclusive club, these are only tiny parts of the whole you; you're much deeper and more valuable than these external factors are defining you as.

There's only one you, so please share that. As you do, this gives others permission to break out of the confines of rigid social values and become more of who they are. When you own who you are and stand in your power, no one can take that away from you. People will always have opinions, yet the more you remain grounded in your truth and own what you know, the less your choices will be questioned. Most people will embrace who you are—and those who continue to judge you at this point are actually judging themselves.

Remember, you're the leader of your own life—guided by your Inner Knowing and strengthened by your personal values. You're exactly where you're supposed to be, so there's no need for catch up. As your mind and body settle into relaxed alertness, your foundation is solid and present. You are able to move forward with your life from where you are right now, rather than from a place of deficit, where you think you *should* be. You no longer need to be swayed by people's opinions or social benchmarks that don't align with your own. Remember, the state of burnout is constrictive and growth prohibitive. Resolving burnout is the process of tuning in to wellness. It's within this state of Grounded Expansion that you build your confidence in your own sense of truth. And it's through the depth of your heartfelt principles that you feel truly driven and alive. This is your WHY, and it feels awesome.

Your personal values help you tap into your energy state. As you connect to the energy of who you are and what you want, you attract more of that—both inside and outside of yourself. More constricted and tense experiences based on misaligned social values and avoidance block and deplete energy, leaving you feeling stuck. However, when you align with your heartfelt principles and tune in to them on deeper levels, you expand your energy state that promotes possibility. Getting acquainted with this energy state takes some practice, and Exercise 29 is a simple way to feel into its pleasurable guidance.

ESSENCE OF YOUR VALUES

Objective:

This meditation will help you tune in to your well of energy and inner guidance by sensing into your chosen personal values that give your mind and body a deeper sense of safety, meaning, and purpose.

Time + Frequency:

Five minutes; at a minimum of three times per week for two weeks (ongoing as needed).

Directions:

STEP 1: Choose a personal value from the list on page 127.

STEP 2: Closing your eyes, begin to quiet down and focus on your breath. Feel yourself present and aware.

STEP 3: Begin to cultivate the lived experience of your chosen value in your body. Imagine how it would feel if you were living it right now and deepen your awareness inward. (If it helps, recall a specific memory when you were living by this personal value.)

STEP 4: Sense into the energetic response of your body. Be with it and explore it with curiosity.

STEP 5: When complete, sit for a few moments in quiet reflection.

Personal Values + Media

Engaging in a life that matters requires living your internal truth and expressing it outward. As you begin to shift your behaviors to align with a life free from burnout, your personal values can be your guide to setting the course for how you want to live. In our age of information overload, your values are a powerful tool to filter out what you no longer want to consume.

Being a conscious consumer of media is beneficial and healthy as you choose what you want to spend your time and energy on. I'm not going to provide a how-to on digital detoxing here, and I suggest that you become aware of the media you take in and begin to notice what aligns with your values and what does not. You may even start to notice that the information you align with feels expansive, interesting, and enlivening. It perhaps sparks your energy and curiosity in a grounded and sustaining way. The information that doesn't align with your values will most likely feel draining and overwhelming. Exercise 30 will help you sort through this process.

Exercise 30

BEING MINDFUL ABOUT MEDIA

Objective:

This exercise is designed to help you get clear on your daily media intake so you can best choose your relationship with media going forward.

Time + Frequency:

Varying over a three-day period; one time (reevaluate as needed).

Directions:

STEP 1: Keep a log of your digital media use for three days.

STEP 2: Along with the platform type, make note of profiles/accounts that align with your values and uplift and inspire. Also make note of those that have the opposite effect.

STEP 3: At the end of the three days, review the log and decide what you want to keep and what you want to release.

STEP 4: Delete connection to all accounts that hinder your well-being.

Whether it's social media, the internet, podcasts, music, movies, books, or some other form, ask yourself why you choose to engage with it. Are your associated thoughts and feelings helpful and uplifting, or not? Remind yourself that choosing to do something just because it's socially valued or to avoid pain exacerbates burnout. To lower burnout risk and enjoy life more, you can choose to unfollow social influencers you don't care about, and if you notice you're on social media to avoid feeling lonely, it may be time to do something else. Call a friend, go for a run, or do one of the many exercises provided in this book to handle those hard moments when you just want to check out.

One more note on this: just as you can burn out on work that you love, it's possible to burn out on media that aligns with your values. Although the mass quantity of what you consume will likely be considerably less once you decide to stop engaging with the stuff that you don't actually care about, it's still important to stay mindful of your media consumption.

Personal Values + Behavior Reframe

Using your personal values as a reference point can also help you reframe activities that you may want or need to do, yet don't have the motivation to engage in. As an example: you want to go to the gym after work. But when the end of the workday comes around, all you can see yourself doing is heading straight home to flop on the couch. You may be able to muster up the motivation by reasoning with yourself, *I'll feel guilty and fat if I don't go* (your why = pain avoidance). A helpful reframe could be that you choose to go to the gym because it aligns with your personal values of physical health and well-being. Both can get you to the gym, but the first tactic is motivating from a more punitive stance, while the second is rooted in empowerment.

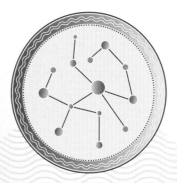

Personal Values + Healthy Boundaries

The desire to avoid pain may have you saying "yes" to a lot more than you want to take on. Setting healthy boundaries and building healthy relationships are vital components of a burnout-free lifestyle. It's about taking responsibility for who you are, what you do, and how you want to be treated. As you become aware of which habits and relationships are helpful and which ones are not, you'll need to make some changes to align with what feels right for you. This means saying "no" to what doesn't align with your personal values and saying "yes" to what does.

Prioritizing your needs based on your values helps you get stable footing as you learn to say "yes" to what you need—even when it goes against social expectations. It's your responsibility to give yourself permission to feel any and all of the emotions that arise, notice and disengage with any unhelpful thoughts, and maintain your choice to set a healthy boundary. This takes real courage, and your personal values will help you stay assured and grounded.

Personal Values + Work

Personal values combined with work can be a challenging area to navigate, yet essential for burnout recovery. Although saying "no" to everything you don't want to do at work would be irresponsible and probably not the best choice professionally, you can set boundaries on things like how much extra work you take on and how many after-work social events you attend. Since burnout is exacerbated at work by an overwhelm of information overload—the push to do more, working with other burnt-out and overextended colleagues and upper managers, and the blurred lines between what's on and off the clock—it's critical to first get clear on what you're willing to say "yes" to, what you prefer to say "no" to, and your reasons why.

TIP

Is my workplace toxic? Just like staying in an unhealthy relationship will tax your resources and put you at further risk of burnout and other mental health issues, so will a toxic work environment. Although quitting your job is not a cure for burnout, if you're experiencing bullying, harassment, gaslighting, or any other acts of aggression toward you—especially if this behavior is coming from the top—it's probably time to find a new job.

The previous sections on media consumption, behavior reframe, and healthy boundaries can all apply to your work environment. Many of my clients felt like they had to say "yes" to everything for fear of not being taken seriously or the risk of losing their jobs. This is where you'll need to use your best judgment within your specific work environment. However, as my clients have experienced from doing this work, any reasonable manager will respect reasonable requests and boundaries, especially when you know what you need and can communicate it with clarity. The mental focus you've acquired through the burnout recovery process and your personal values will help set you up for the important work conversations you'll need to have in order to make a positive impact.

The practice of boundary setting frees people of the belief that there is not enough time in the day to take a break or do something they really want for themselves. Whether it's boundary setting at work or within your personal life, creating time for rest and saying "yes" to what you really want is a requirement for burnout recovery. Even the thought of boundary setting can be terrifying, yet it gets much easier (and liberating) with practice. Exercise 31 will help you plan ahead so you can begin setting effective boundaries.

BECOMING A BOUNDARY-SETTING EXPERT

Objective:

You'll devise and execute a plan to set an important boundary in your life that will support a burnout-free lifestyle.

Time + Frequency:

Fifteen minutes to devise with variable execution time; a minimum of one time before moving on to the next chapter (repeat often to gain mastery).

Directions:

Answer the the prompts on the opposite page to complete your action plan.

1. What is something or someone that you would benefit from setting a boundary with?

2. Which personal values support this choice?

3. What will you do or say to set this boundary?

4. When and where will you do it?

5. What uncomfortable emotions do you anticipate will come up for you?

6. What may be some good feeling emotions that will arise as a result?

7. What are some avoidant or discouraging thoughts you may have?

8. How will you manage your emotions and thoughts?

Chapter Summary

Life can be fun—and you deserve to feel inspired and available to live the life you want. Society has its overarching set of rules, guidelines, and norms that influence how we as social beings live. Although these social values aren't inherently good or bad, if they do not align with your personal values, you will buy into a system that conflicts with who you are. And since we live in a burnout culture, if you keep living by the values that perpetuate burnout, you'll remain susceptible to it.

Rethinking what's right for you—even if that means going against the grain—can create its own kind of conflict. You'll have to be willing to show up for all of your emotions in the face of difficult choices and conversations. Getting clear on your personal values strengthens your resolve to stick with this change process and build a truly purposeful life.

Living your personal values is both an internal, energetic resonance of *Yes, this is my truth* and an outward expression of how you choose to schedule and move through your day. Each informs the other as you cultivate a deep sense of inner truth that's reflected into your outer world. This path isn't easy, especially at the beginning, but the more you show up for yourself, the more inner trust and power will support your outer experiences.

As with all aspects of change, you have to rewire your body and mind into this new normal. You're releasing the unnecessary busyness, excessive seriousness, pressure to be there for others while neglecting your needs, and other rules of adulting. You're now able to define your own milestones and consciously choose how you want to interact with media, within interpersonal relationships, at work, and more. You get to be *you*—constantly evolving as you heal and grow, letting your personal values lead the way.

Chapter Skill Take-Aways

Your personal values, or heartfelt principles, help you sense into what matters to you. The practices in this chapter help move your body and mind out of the misaligned social values that have driven your past so that you can more fully embrace your new future.

- Exercise 26 *Reworking Busyness* and Exercise 27 *Encouraging Silliness* help your body and mind move out of the habitual ways that make adult life harder and less fun. I recommend practicing *Reworking Busyness* daily for at least a week, as you connect to the experience of having plenty to do (being busy) without the "busyness" of the daily grind. You can do *Encouraging Silliness* at any time and for as long as you want to practice.

- Exercise 28 *Getting Clear on Your "Why"* prepares you to practice and live a life that is deeply meaningful to you. You're getting acquainted with your body's inner resonance with Exercise 29 *Essence of Your Values* meditation. From this sense of clarity of what you want, why you want it, and how good it feels to live aligned with your personal values, you can navigate the many aspects of today's fast-paced and information-overloaded burnout culture. Exercise 30 *Being Mindful about Media* is one concrete way to become a conscious consumer of what matters and what's healthy for you.

- Exercise 31 *Becoming a Boundary-Setting Expert* is a vital skill to resolve burnout and create an ongoing burnout-free lifestyle. By taking your personal values into consideration, it provides added fortitude to set important boundaries despite incredibly uncomfortable emotions and unhelpful thoughts that will naturally arise as part of the change process. This exercise is designed to integrate the skills and concepts you've learned in this book so far and can be used as a guide for all areas in your life where you need to say "no" to others so you can truly say "yes" to your health and well-being. I highly recommend that you execute this plan at least once before moving on to the final chapter.

Chapter 6

Wellness Focus

Make yourself some tea and settle in, because this chapter is all about nurturing yourself. I realized that my own healing journey was about showing up for myself every day to the best of my ability—lovingly realizing that "my best self" varied, given the day or even the moment. So, allowing whatever version of your best self to exist in the current moment is enough.

Knowing what your best is on any given day requires being fully honest with yourself, and this level of honesty and self-trust isn't about being perfect. It begins when you can admit that you don't know everything and are ready to open up to this learning, healing, and growing process. The more you trust yourself, the more your daily best provides healing space to become who you are.

Mantras Revisited

A mantra, affirmation, or reframe is only effective when you believe it to be true, or you believe in the potential of its truth. That's when adding an introductory phrase to a mantra can be very helpful, such as:

I'm ready to _____

or

I'm learning to _____

It's like placing training wheels on your bike; you can always remove them as you gain confidence. When working with big concepts like self-trust and deep honesty, these trainers could be something like this: *I'm ready to trust my Inner Knowing* or *I'm learning to be completely honest with myself.* Say these to yourself and notice how they shift your sense of possibility.

TIP

Being honest with yourself may seem obvious, yet like all of healing, it's an ever-deepening practice. Since your reptilian brain and much of your subconscious is designed to protect you, it's easy to lie to yourself. But as you practice honesty and truth, you'll uncover and dismantle everything that doesn't support your healthiest and highest potential.

Anything's possible when you let go of all the things you think are keeping you safe—but are limiting your potential. As you step into the honest awesomeness of who you truly are, you become an unstoppable source of Inner Knowing. No longer guided by fear, shame, doubt, or the need to prove yourself, you get to be you. Knowing that you're fluid and ever-changing makes you available for true transformation.

Life is happening all around you, and it's up to *you* to decide how you want to maneuver through the world. Whether you're walking down the street with your partner, out with friends, spending time with family, or at work, you are simultaneously navigating internal and external stimuli. If you ignore your Inner Knowing and fully identify with the outer world, your true self will get muddled and lost. Burnout recovery and sustained well-being is a process of learning to be with the ups and downs of the day, without losing sight of your internal guiding force.

Remember, Inner Knowing is the deep trust that comes when you recognize that all aspects of who you are want what's best for you. Yes, you may have unhelpful thoughts and engage in self-sabotaging

behavior from time to time, but even these tactics were intended to help and protect you. You are your own advocate, and even if you slip into old habits on occasion, your deeper truth will help you make conscious decisions to support wellness.

Wellness isn't simply about self-preservation—it's about fully living up to your potential in your most honest and true way. This book has been designed to set you up for the practice of aligning all aspects of yourself. We started with the body, and you're encouraged to return to your body as often as possible because it's where emotions reside and where you can turn your attention away from disorganized and unhelpful thinking. As your safe base, you can settle into the acknowledgment of you, as a whole being, in the present moment. Exercise 32 brings this all together.

GUIDED INTO WHOLENESS

Objective:

This practice connects you to all the aspects of yourself in present moment awareness to deepen your sense of wholeness.

Time + Frequency:

Six to eight minutes; one time daily for two weeks (ongoing as needed).

Directions:

STEP 1: Sit quietly with your eyes closed and begin to notice your physical body. Through your internal awareness, scan your whole body and breathe into the tension areas and then release. Ease your posture into a comfortable yet upright position. Be with this experience for about one minute.

STEP 2: Become aware of your emotional state and sense into it within your body. Remain present as the observer of your emotions and return your focus to these sensations in your body whenever your mind wanders. Be with this experience for about one minute.

STEP 3: Now notice your mind and continue to use it as an awareness tool to remain present within your being. When you become aware of a thought taking you into the past or future, return your focus to what's happening now. Be with this experience for about one minute.

STEP 4: Going deeper into your body, choose a personal value (see page 127) and be with the energy of your heartfelt principle. If helpful, recall a time when you were living this value. Be with this experience for about one minute.

STEP 5: While in this heartfelt state, notice your thoughts, emotions, and physical body. Be with all of it and stay with this whole presence for one to two minutes.

STEP 6: To finish, say to yourself, *I am whole, I am well.* Then spend a few moments in quiet reflection of your practice.

You cannot change what happened yesterday, nor can you control what will happen tomorrow. Yet, you can decide to act today on something that happened yesterday or set plans for tomorrow. As you learn to trust yourself, start with the present moment, which is all you really have. Settle into your body, feel the feels, watch your thoughts, and align your Inner Knowing with your personal values to simultaneously ground and expand with your sense of wholeness. The more familiar you become with feeling "whole," the more honest and trusting of yourself you will become.

Rethinking Self-Care

Having no regrets or desiring for the past to have been different frees your thoughts, emotions, and intended actions to be present and move you forward. You become the conscious creator of your life as you engage fully in the flow of "now," which is always in motion. Time, speed, and pace are all relative, and when you slow down to "catch your breath" you can move with the natural rhythms of your life.

Even as the world seems to fly by at lightning speed, you now realize that "going faster" doesn't always mean "getting more done"—it actually means you're missing out on life because you're so busy trying to reach some imaginary finish line that's just out of sight. When you align your internal rhythms with a pace that feels more like inner peace, you "keep up" in all the ways that are important to you: your bills are paid, the laundry gets done, and your resume still looks impressive. From here, you can be with yourself in a way that's sustainable, manageable, and meaningful.

When you learn to truly be with yourself, the internal structures that have kept you stuck and burnt out fade away. As you pay attention to what's really going on, you get to make informed decisions on how you want to treat yourself. This self-care is a culmination of treating yourself well, speaking kindly to yourself, and allowing all of your emotions to rise to the surface.

The Platinum Rule of Self-Care

Self-care is the empowered act of choosing how you want to treat yourself. The "golden rule" is: Treat *others* as you want to be treated. And the "platinum rule" is: Treat *yourself* as you want to be treated. When you honor the platinum rule, you can fully show up for yourself, which in turn lets you show up for others.

Self-care helps you recognize and do what's is best for you. Recall the three-word mantra, "I choose _____ from Exercise 4 (see page 20). This mantra honors that you have a choice in how you treat yourself and are autonomous in your decision making. To support your ongoing self-care, remember that self-care is a lifestyle choice, so you must get fully comfortable with choosing *you*. Exercise 33 is offered as an ongoing practice to deepen your ability to lovingly care for yourself.

I honestly believe that the kindest thing you can do for everyone involved is prioritize your need for self-care. When you're well rested, clearheaded, and feeling joyful and fulfilled, you can care for others from a deep place of connection. Conversely, when you're stressed out and stretched thin, you're functioning in survival mode. This can leave you feeling disconnected and saying "yes" to people out of obligation and to avoid conflict. As you learn to be present and loving toward yourself, you can connect more with the people and things you really care about.

Being honest and self-respecting enables you to treat others with the same level of dignity. When you align your actions with your values, you are making room for all of your emotions, including the delicious ones! When you speak kindly to

"I CHOOSE ME" MANTRA MEDITATION

Objective:

In a society that has taught you to place everyone else's needs before your own, this mantra meditation rewires your body and mind to accept and embrace a new paradigm of self-care.

Time + Frequency:

Three to five minutes; two times per d ay for two weeks (recommended as an ongoing daily practice).

Directions:

STEP 1: Be quiet with yourself, ground into your body, and become aware of all of you.

STEP 2: With your eyes closed or open, begin to repeat the mantra, *I choose me.*

STEP 3: Notice any thoughts and emotions that arise.

STEP 4: Return your focus to your mantra (each return is a "thought reframe").

STEP 5: As you continue to repeat this mantra, cultivate the inner tone of your self-care values.

STEP 6: Keep going and be with this experience.

STEP 7: To finish, end the mantra and sit with your experience in self-reflection.

yourself and return to your body as a safe base, something really magical happens as you reclaim yourself and feel grounded and at home wherever you are. Since picking up this book, you've been practicing a holistic approach to self-care, allowing all of you to be seen and nurtured. Let's consider now how self-care has already positively impacted your life by using Exercise 34 to reflect on your healing process.

By making *you* a priority in your own life, you allow the outside actions of self-care to heal your deeper levels of being. Although activities like getting a manicure, a massage, or a facial may fall under the category of "self-care," if done without intention or presence they are only skin-deep and won't help you recover from burnout. Yet there are ways you can make this type of self-care truly transformative.

For example, if you love going to the spa, consider making it a deep healing experience. Instead of being on your phone or flipping through magazines as your toes are being polished, you can remain present in the comfortable chair, give gratitude for the person taking care of your feet, and appreciate the time you've given yourself to be quiet and receive. Self-care is when you can give to yourself for no other reason than to be nurtured in the present moment.

THEN AND NOW (JOURNAL PROMPTS)

Objective:
Through two writing prompts, this exercise is designed for self-reflection and acknowledgment of your progress thus far.

Time + Frequency:
Fifteen minutes; one time (revisit as needed).

Directions:
STEP 1: Set about fifteen minutes aside to be quiet and reflective. Read and consider the following inquiries:

1. Since the first day I engaged with this book, how has my relationship with my body, emotions, thoughts, energy, and Inner Knowing changed?

2. Since the first day I engaged with this book, how has my relationship with my outer world changed?

STEP 2: Write down your responses in your journal or in another analog source. Reread your responses and then do an act of celebration for all of your healing so far.

Small Steps in the Moment = Evolving Transformation

Yes, we want transformation now! But think about it this way: you're already in the process of transformation. Every decision you make, thought you think, and emotion you feel now is you changing. There's no benefit to wishing your past were different or trying to speed up time to be your future self. Regardless of the choices you made in the past, you're exactly who and where you're supposed to be in this very moment—as you learn how to become who you will be.

As you become increasingly aware of all of the external messaging of who people think you are and how you're supposed to be, you get to choose what you know to be right for you. External forces—often with contradicting messages—create a sense of internal chaos and confusion. This is how deepening your trust in your own knowing, understanding your "why," and honoring yourself are the most valuable guiding principles to take step-by-step actions in your wellness transformation.

This all happens through present moment awareness as you honor the balance of "rest" and "action" and find your own pace. All of the exercises in this book are designed to facilitate productive rest so you can be fully present and purposeful in your life. Exercise 35 reviews all of the exercises so far in this book, giving you a chance to reflect on how far you've come.

TIP

Recalling Exercise 6 *Boosting Gratitude* from chapter 1 (see page 36), use the same method to practice being grateful for you. Say, *I get to be me* a few times. Feel into it and see how grateful you can feel for the opportunity to be you!

COMPLETE LIST OF EXERCISES FOR REVIEW AND REFLECTION

Objective:

This activity accounts for all thirty-four exercises you've learned in this book until now, with the intention to review and reflect on your experience with these practices to resolve burnout and cultivate a lifestyle that sustains your well-being.

Time + Frequency:

Twenty minutes; one time (return to review and reflect on your self-healing trajectory).

Directions:

STEP 1: Review the list of exercises from each chapter (opposite).

STEP 2: Spend time recalling your practice for each one.

STEP 3: Consider which exercises you're most drawn to and why.

STEP 4: Consider which exercises could become part of your daily routine to support a burnout-free lifestyle.

Introduction: What is Burnout and Do I Suffer from It?

1. *Burnout Symptoms Self-Assessment*
2. *Your Stress Tigers*
3. *Reclaim Yourself*
4. *Three-Word Mantra*

Chapter 1: Mindfulness Focus

5. *Monotasking*
6. *Boosting Gratitude*
7. *Learning to Activate Your Vagus Nerve*

Chapter 2: Body Focus

8. *Grounded Expansion*
9. *Body-Awareness Meditation*
10. *Determining Your HtBR*
11. *Freeze Frame Awareness*
12. *Body-Focused Breathing*
13. *Breathing Slower*
14. *Create Your Own Burnout Metaphor and Release Strategy*

Chapter 3: Mind Focus

15. *I Don't Have Enough ...*
16. *Spiraling Up!*
17. *Rewire Your Brain*
18. *Phasing "Should" Out of Your Life*
19. *Mindful Slow-Mo*

Chapter 4: Emotion Focus

20. *Emotion Identification + Root Relations*
21. *Releasing Emotions*
22. *Body + Mind as Allies to Process Fear*
23. *Can I Get a Witness?*
24. *Practice Breathing Well*
25. *Uplevel Your Mood to Uplevel Your Life*

Chapter 5: Social + Personal Focus

26. *Reworking Busyness*
27. *Encouraging Silliness*
28. *Getting Clear on Your "Why"*
29. *Essence of Your Values*
30. *Being Mindful about Media*
31. *Becoming a Boundary-Setting Expert*

Chapter 6: Wellness Focus

32. *Guided into Wholeness*
33. *"I Choose Me" Mantra Meditation*
34. *Then and Now (Journal Prompts)*

Wellness beyond burnout is the creation of habits that over time, and with consistent practice, they become your new way of being. Your wellness goal isn't something to check off a to-do list, but rather a new way of relating to your whole self and being within the world. This is accomplished by becoming increasingly aware of your present moment experience as you choose what feels right to you. Paying attention to the underlying motivators of each moment you can ask yourself, *Does this "why" support my well-being?* If the answer is "no," lovingly release it and choose again by making necessary changes either in this exact moment or over time. The more you align your daily life with a focus on wellness, the more sustained it becomes.

TIP

What do I need right now? is a great question to ask yourself to stay focused on wellness and gain clarity on next-step actions. It could be as simple as drinking a glass of water or taking three deep breaths. Whatever it is, self-inquiry can offer valuable insight.

Sustained wellness doesn't mean that you'll feel great all the time or never struggle again. It's about truly showing up for yourself in every moment exactly as you are. From this conscious place of acceptance, you can then choose your next self-care step. The healing process of being human doesn't end when this book does.

These tools and concepts are just the beginning of your next cycle of personal exploration, healing, and growth. In order to fully embrace a burnout-free lifestyle, you must practice it until it becomes your new normal. When it becomes habit, you can continue to heal and evolve through your holistic approach to present moment awareness of your own experience. By continuing to cultivate your Inner Knowing, the depth of your potential and what you can accomplish in your lifetime are limitless. The only barrier is *you*, so it's important to understand your body's response to stress and change, pay attention to your inner dialogue and beliefs, and notice how your thoughts interact with your emotions. This awareness will help keep you aligned with your values that support optimal wellness.

In Exercise 36 *Your Continuing Wellness Plan* (see pages 150 to 151), you'll create activities that will support your ongoing healing and evolving sense of well-being by mapping out your daily productive rest practice. There are many exercises to choose from, but the important thing is to devise a practice that's manageable and spread out through your day to ensure you don't fall back into the habit of steamrolling through a hectic day. If you do this, you'll relapse—and I know you don't want that. Moving forward, you'll need to remain vigilant with your practice—not in a strict, beat-yourself-up kind of way, but in a way that sets you up for self-accountability and aligns with your personal values (i.e., because you want to!).

In this way, your "why" becomes bigger than a few exercises you do every day. This plan is truly getting you to choose self-care in all areas of your life. You do it not only to prevent burnout from returning, but also because it feels good to feel good. It feels empowering and motivating to be energized, enlivened, confident, and connected. Knowing and trusting yourself is liberating. I encouraged you to keep with it.

You have thirty-four exercises in this book to choose from—pick the ones that feel right and most beneficial for you. Remember, this can change as you change, heal, and evolve, so choose the exercises according to your growth. The important thing is to stay consciously aware of what you need now without buying into unhelpful thoughts that may tell you that you no longer need to practice—we all need to practice on strengthening what we want to focus on and pruning the rest. What do you want to focus on? As you complete *Your Continuing Wellness Plan*, choose wisely and be well.

YOUR CONTINUING WELLNESS PLAN

Objective:

This exercise helps you create a daily set of awareness activities to sustain a holistic sense of who you are, even in the midst of a busy workday.

Time + Frequency:

Fifteen minutes to devise; one time to set up and to be done daily; ongoing review and execution based on shifting needs/desires.

Directions:

Review the list of exercises and your responses from Exercise 35 on page 147, then create your continuing wellness plan, guided by the following questions.

What exercise(s) will I do before work each day?

What exercise(s) will I do to make sure I have at least three mini-breaks during each workday?

(Do I need to set an alert on my phone as a reminder to ensure I do them?)

     Yes   No

What after-work exercise(s) will I do to help me decompress after work and get quality sleep?

What external obstacles may get in the way of this plan? How can I overcome them?

What internal obstacles may get in the way of this plan? How can I overcome them?

My "Why": What personal values align with my reason to stick with this daily practice?

The date I will start this plan is: _____

and I hold myself accountable now _____
(*initials*)

Further, if you're feeling called to reread this book, I recommend doing it. You're in a new place physically, mentally, emotionally, and energetically. Because of this, you'll be able to take in the information in a new way and deepen your practice. Many of my clients who finish the digital eight-week program, Say Goodbye to Burnout, and having successfully resolved their burnout opt to restart the full practice from week one in order to reinforce what they've learned. They have reported a greater understanding of the work and in turn of themselves, building an ever-enhancing sense of wellness.

You Are Your Wellness Guide

Your Inner Knowing is your wellness guide; it sparks the fire and lights the path so you can keep burning bright. By being an active participant with this book, you've been learning how to tune in to your inner sense of knowing. Your body, mind, emotions, and deeper energetics of your values feed the flame as you become grounded and expansive from the inside out.

Recall that at the beginning of this book you tapped into your visceral experience of burnout, and then you began to practice loosening its grip. Exercise 37 *Your Virtual Reality = Future Wellness Now* offers the opportunity to explore the visceral experience of full-on expansion and healing potential as you imagine stepping into your future self. Even if you feel the remnants of burnout, allow this whole-being practice to be your reminder of what's possible—as your inner wisdom guides your healing.

Settling into the sense of who you are now brings safety, stability, and expansion that enables you to consciously change, grow, and evolve. It provides the sustenance and support to help you fully relax into being you. Each time you return to this place of Inner Knowing, you're reinforcing that you're safe. The better you feel from the inside out, the more aligned you'll be with your whole self—the expanding fullness of who you are and who you're becoming.

Being your whole self requires daily practice of returning to it with present awareness. Every moment is an opportunity to regain focus and be with yourself as you engage with life in the most honest way you can. It's not a forced thing, but it's a release of preconceived notions enabling you to tap into the true essence of your depth.

Trusting your inner guidance system is you practicing wellness in everyday life. It's a choice you can make in each moment. When you notice old habits or unhelpful thoughts creep in, remember to return your focus to your Inner Knowing. Everyday life is the ideal platform to practice well-being: engage with life, be present in your body as often as possible, treat yourself with kindness, and let your Inner Knowing be your wellness guide.

YOUR VIRTUAL REALITY = FUTURE WELLNESS NOW

Objective:

The power of visualization is taken to the next level in this exercise as you ground into your body and step into your new life of ever-expanding optimal wellness and possibility.

Time + Frequency:

Fifteen minutes; three times per week for two weeks (ongoing as needed).

Directions:

STEP 1: Recall the second prompt of Exercise 3 *Reclaim Yourself* (see page 17) that asks, "Who am I without stress?" and answer the following:

How does my body feel?

What kind of thoughts do I have?

What are the predominant emotions that arise?

How do they align with my heartfelt principles?

STEP 2: Now, decide on a situation where you could be experiencing this in real life. While seated with your eyes closed, imagine that you're putting on a virtual reality headset, and you see yourself in first person in the dream situation of your choice.

Answer the following questions:

1. What do you see? How do you move? Feel free to move around in this virtual reality. Be this reality—it's yours.

2. How does your body feel? Sense and relax into it.

3. What are you thinking about? Keep thinking these helping, loving, abundant thoughts!

4. What is your emotional state? Let it be uplifting and elevate the intensity of these feel-good feels.

5. What is the experience like as you align with your values? Deeply enjoy your tuned-in energy.

6. Continue being in this space with all of you, as all of you, embodying your wellness.

STEP 3: When you're ready to return to the world at hand, allow the virtual reality device to turn off and fade to black.

STEP 4: With your eyes still closed, be in this new state as you continue to sense into your experience.

STEP 5: To finish, open your eyes into the next new moment.

Chapter Summary

You made it! Let's take a moment and celebrate. Well done!! Keep celebrating, keep evolving, and keep being you in the present moment. As you explore your potential in daily living by showing up as honest as possible for yourself, you will build an unshakable trust in your ability to be and do anything that you want—without feeling burnt out. There truly is no limit to your potential.

Self-care isn't skin deep, nor is it a luxury. Everyone can practice self-care, no matter one's socioeconomic status. Yes, we each have our own unique life circumstances and internal obstacles to work with. And we each have the ability to choose how we want to treat ourselves. This makes us more present to our own needs and more present for the people and things that matter to us. Loving yourself is the most loving thing you can do for another person. You show up fully for both of you, giving them permission to do the same.

By choosing *you*, you're going against social norms, which builds resiliency to keep being yourself. As you continue to honor "rest" as much as "action" and practice your daily awareness exercises to release old conditioning and become more "present moment aware," you stay grounded in your being and expand into more of who you are. This is no small feat; however, as you've been learning through the process of burnout recovery, it's doable. So, keep with it because the more you do it, the easier it becomes to show up as you with ease and drive.

The healing and evolving process is naturally an uncertain and ever-changing one, but the more flexible you are (i.e., being with all of your emotions, choosing helpful thoughts that support self-kindness, and tuning in to your heartfelt desires housed within your body), the more available you'll be as the conscious creator of your change process. Remember, *you* are your own wellness guide, and the more you practice and trust your Inner Knowing, the more you'll expand into your fullest human potential.

Chapter Skill Take-Aways

This chapter's tools have brought together the themes of each chapter and prepared you for next-step actions in your continuing wellness journey. These exercises, along with all of the practices in this book, are designed to support a burnout-free lifestyle as you heal on deepening levels and excel at whatever life ambitions you choose.

- Exercise 32 *Guided into Wholeness* is a practice that explores present moment awareness of your whole being. It helps cultivate a sense of grounded presence and wellness that reinforces each aspect of you as an ally of the whole.

- By practicing Exercise 33 *"I Choose Me" Mantra Meditation*, you're reinforcing your choice for self-care and actively removing subconscious blocks and deflating emotions that attempt to protect you from yourself.

- Exercise 34 *Then and Now (Journal Prompts)* and Exercise 35 *Complete List of Exercises for Review and Reflection* are both exercises in recognizing where you were at the start of this healing journey, how far you've come, and how daily practice of productive rest deepens your connection to your sense of self both internally and within the social environment.

- Taking into consideration all that you have learned and practiced, Exercise 36 *Your Continuing Wellness Plan* provides you with a personalized road map to keep up with your daily practice as you complete this book and current healing cycle. I encourage you to restart this book and engage with it again whenever you feel called to do so. Both the reread and the practice of Exercise 37 *Your Virtual Reality = Future Wellness Now* will prepare you for an ever-deepening experience of healing and optimal wellness.

Acknowledgments

At the start of this book writing adventure I chose the mantra, "This book has already written itself," which helped me stay focused, feel enlivened, and trust in the process. During the final reread, with the bulk of the work now done, and having turned out so beautifully, I said to myself, "This book really did write itself." It did! And, I couldn't have done it without the support of many people and influences.

To say I am thrilled with the results is an understatement. The entire Rock Point team at Quarto Publishing, especially Group Publisher Rage Kindelsperger, who helped bring my knowledge out in a clear, colorful, and honest way. I give enormous thanks to Creative Director Laura Drew and Designer Evelin Kasikov for making these pages so beautiful. To John Foster, my Editor, who at times I joked was my burnout prevention coach, provided the expertise and assurance to help keep my stress levels in check and my perseverance high. John, thank goodness you know how to move a book along from inception to publication, and I'm humbly grateful for your guidance.

From the early stages through to the final edits, my friend and colleague Lauren Lascher was there for me. Bringing my first pages to you, it was your belief in me and your ability to see through my choppy and disorganized draft that kept me from throwing it in the garbage and quitting. From offering your beach house as a haven to do the third-round rewrites to all the moments in between, thank you for your true friendship and support.

Celebrating successes before they began, Jennifer Brick and Sarah Mac saw this book into completion long before I did. Your ability to hold that vision for me, along with your encouraging words and feedback, even when I wasn't feeling so hot about it all, gave me the boost to stay grateful for the opportunity to share my work in written form and to remember to have fun doing it.

And, speaking of fun, Liz Moran, special events planner, kept me inspired with book release party ideas since before the contract was even signed. Along the way she has been my check-in buddy and a huge supporter of my work. Liz, I'm grateful for our friendship and your expertise. Thank you in advance for the exceptional book launch party.

Look, Ma, I wrote a book! From five thousand miles away and phone calls while I walked through Central Park for a breather and evening calls when I needed to feel safe and supported, Mom and Dad, you were one hundred percent there for me. You have been the solid foundation I knew I could count on during the ups and downs of this whole process. It's been beautifully healing and life-affirming. Thank you.

I want to send a shout-out and special big thanks to Clare Wesley, the most compassionate, fierce, and real woman I know. As my therapist, she guided me through my twenties and showed me that I have options. That I get to choose how I want to think, feel, and take action. Thank you, Clare, for helping me heal from depression and laying the groundwork for the knowledge provided within these pages.

It was the aid of Clare in my healing journey that inspired my decision to receive a master's degree in social work so that I could help people make important changes in their lives as Clare did for me. Participating in the National Child Traumatic Stress Network Demonstration Project while studying social work at Fordham University, I gained experiential knowledge of how chronic stress impacts the brain and nervous system. Simultaneously reading Bessel van der Kolk's book, *The Body Keeps the Score*, my eyes were opened to the vast healing potential of body-mind integration.

I became infinitely inspired to learn everything I could about this holistic approach to healing and optimal wellness. I'm grateful to all of my professors at Fordham University, Bessel van der Kolk and his research team, along with many other thought leaders within this expansive field of inquiry. These innovators who have strongly impacted my vision of wellness and how I support people within their healing process include: Bruce Lipton, Candace Pert, Deepak Chopra, Louise Hay, Brené Brown, Dawson Church, Jill Bolte Taylor, Russ Harris, Jon Kabat-Zinn, Pema Chödrön, Christiane Northrup, Mona Lisa Shulz, Joan Borysenko, and the HeartMath Institute.

The people, teams, and organizations that have shaped my personal healing and professional journey could go on for pages and continues to grow. For now I will stop here, and with deep appreciation say thank you for all that you have taught me, will teach me, and the healing influence you have had, and continue to have, on so many people.

Lastly, yet certainly not leastly, I want to thank YOU. I feel so honored to have been able to create this book and that you have chosen to engage with it for your own well-being. Thank you for supporting my work, for trusting in the healing benefits encased in this book, and for showing up to your own healing process. I wish you continued wellness and growth potential!!

About the Author

Charlene Rymsha, LCSW, is the founder of Everyday Coherence, a psychotherapist, holistic lifestyle coach, and creator of the Say Goodbye to Burnout method. She lives in NYC and helps ambitious and creative professionals overcome burnout without sacrificing their relationships, paycheck, or freedom. Clients, from virtually everywhere, arrive to Charlene on edge, unfocused, and exhausted and are seeking to regain their confidence, clarity, and strength. Through formal training in clinical social work, mindfulness, and somatic modalities, Charlene brings an integrative and proven approach to the burnout recovery process with a compassionate and evidence-based system of support. We all deserve to live a life full of joy and meaning, and the Say Goodbye to Burnout method enables those who are suffering to regain joyful connected relationships and professional success. This is Charlene's first book, offering a comprehensive guide to burn bright (not out).

Photo by Amy Keum

You can find added resources that supplement this book at: *everydaycoherence.com/burnbright*

You can learn more about Charlene and how to work with her at: *everydaycoherence.com*

Index